MacBrayne Ships

Alistair Deayton

AMBERLEY

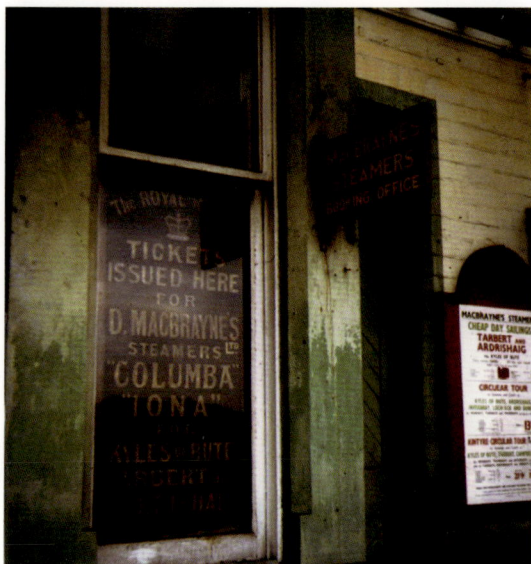

The MacBrayne office on Rothesay Pier in the 1950s, still advertising sailings by *Columba* and *Iona* some twenty years or so after they were scrapped.

First published 2014

Amberley Publishing
The Hill, Stroud
Gloucestershire, GL5 4EP

www.amberley-books.com

Copyright © Alistair Deayton, 2014

The right of Alistair Deayton to be identified as the Author of this work has been asserted in accordance with the Copyrights, Designs and Patents Act 1988.

ISBN 978-1-4456-3582-8 (print)
ISBN 978-1-4456-3598-9 (ebook)

British Library Cataloguing in Publication Data.
A catalogue record for this book is available from the British Library.

Typeset in 11pt on 12pt Sabon LT Std.
Typesetting by Amberley Publishing.
Printed in the UK.

CONTENTS

David Hutcheson.

David MacBrayne.

INTRODUCTION

The name of David MacBrayne was synonymous with shipping services in the West Highlands and Islands for almost a hundred years, from 1879 until the formation of Caledonian MacBrayne in 1973.

Our story starts in 1851, when George and James Burns sold their steamer services to the West Highlands, along with the steamers, to David Hutcheson and his brother Alexander, with the proviso that they took on David MacBrayne, a nephew of the Burns brothers, as a junior partner. In 1876 and 1878 respectively the Hutcheson brothers retired and MacBrayne took over the company, running it under his own name from the following year. In 1905 David MacBrayne retired at the age of ninety-one and David MacBrayne Ltd was incorporated, run by his son David Hope MacBrayne. In 1928, following the loss of three major units of the fleet in the previous year, *Sheila*, *Chevalier* and *Grenadier*, the company was on the verge of bankruptcy and, following government intervention, a new entity was formed to operate the services, 50 per cent owned by the London, Midland & Scottish Railway, and 50 per cent by Coast Lines Ltd. In 1948, with railway nationalisation, the LMS half was taken over by British Railways and, in 1969, became part of the Scottish Transport Group, with the Coast Lines share coming under public ownership later that year. 1973 saw the merger with the Clyde operator Caledonian Steam Packet Ltd to form Caledonian MacBrayne, which continues operating west coast ferry services to this day.

Over the years a small number of independent operators were taken over by Hutcheson and MacBrayne, including the Glasgow & Lochfine (sic) Steam Packet Co. in 1857; John Ramsay and others, operating services to Islay, in 1876; the Loch Leven Shipping Company Ltd in 1911; Alexander Paterson of Oban in 1934; and McCallum Orme Ltd on 1 January 1948. With the takeover of Williamson-Buchanan Steamers by the LMSR in 1935, the two long-distance turbine steamers *Queen Alexandra* and *King George V* were absorbed into the MacBrayne fleet. The Clyde & Campbeltown Shipping Co. Ltd was controlled by David MacBrayne Ltd from March 1937 and its steamers took on the MacBrayne funnel, but it continued as a separate operation.

From the outset a wide variety of steamers were built, from small cargo steamers that could traverse the Crinan Canal to magnificent paddle steamers for the Royal Route from Glasgow to Ardrishaig and screw steamers with sleeping accommodation for the long route from Glasgow to Stornoway. From the late 1880s to the turn of the century a succession of second-hand steamers were purchased, and in the early years of the twentieth century some of the first motor vessels to be operated in the British Isles were built for the company. The new ownership in the 1930s saw the introduction of a series of larger motor vessels, including a couple with diesel-electric propulsion. 1964 saw the arrival of the first trio of car ferries, built, like the Clyde trio of ten years previously, with lift loading of cars.

This volume illustrates the vast majority of the 129 vessels operated by Hutcheson and MacBrayne in the 121 years from 1851 to 1972.

Chapter 1

DAVID HUTCHESON & CO.: 1851–78

When David Hutcheson, in partnership with his brother Alexander and David MacBrayne, took over the West Highland services of G. & J. Burns in 1851, he took over the following eight steamers:

Curlew (1837), operating from Inverness to Cromarty, Invergordon, Burghead and Little Ferry.

Shandon (1839), a wooden-hulled steamer on the Crinan to Oban service.

Duntroon Castle (1842), a survivor from the Glasgow Castle Steam Packet Company, which had dominated the route in the 1830s and early 1840s, operating from Glasgow to Oban, Tobermory, and Portree, extended to Gairloch in the summer months.

Dolphin (1844), operating out of Oban three days a week to Staffa and Iona and three days a week to Fort William. She was sold for blockade running in 1862.

Edinburgh Castle (1844), another survivor of the Glasgow Castle Steam Packet Company, operating on the Caledonian Canal thrice weekly in each direction. She was renamed *Glengarry* in 1875 and continued on the route until broken up in 1927 at the grand old age of eighty-three.

Pioneer (1844), built for the Railway Steam Packet Co. Ltd for rail-connected services from Greenock, purchased by Messrs Burns in 1847 and placed on the Glasgow to Ardrishaig service. *Pioneer* remained in the fleet until scrapped in 1895, latterly being on the Sound of Mull service from Oban from 1881 until withdrawn in 1893.

Sisters *Cygnet* and *Lapwing* (both 1848), operating from Glasgow to Inverness via the Crinan and Caledonian canals. *Lapwing* was sunk in 1859, but *Cygnet* survived until wrecked in 1882. These were an unusual shape, with rounded bows and inset paddles to fit the locks of the Crinan Canal, probably similar to the 'fiddle-steamers' of Sweden, designed to fit the locks of the Göta Canal, of which a replica, *Eric Nordevall II*, has been built in recent years.

In addition, there were two horse-drawn track boats operating on the Crinan Canal from Ardrishaig to Crinan, *Maid of Perth* and *Sunbeam* (1847). These operated until succeeded by *Linnet* in 1866. The term 'Royal Route' had been applied to the service from Glasgow to Ardrishaig, and on through the Crinan Canal to Crinan and northwards to Oban, Fort William and Inverness, since Queen Victoria had travelled on the route in 1847, and it was used in marketing by the company for the next 100 years or more, until long after the Ardrishaig to Inverness sector had been taken over by motor buses.

Hutcheson's first new steamer was *Mountaineer*, built in 1852 for the Ardrishaig service, which enabled *Pioneer* to move to the Crinan to Oban route and the old *Shandon* to be withdrawn and sold for use in Australia.

Another new paddle steamer, *Chevalier*, entered the fleet in 1853, running from Glasgow to Oban and Skye via the Mull of Kintyre, with the service extended on occasion to Stornoway and Scrabster. She replaced *Duntroon Castle*, which was sold and used on the Newhaven to Dieppe service. *Chevalier*, sadly, was wrecked in the Sound of Jura on 24 November 1854.

In 1855, David Hutcheson & Co. was awarded its first Royal Mail contract, thus entitling the steamers to be prefixed RMS and the company to advertise itself as 'Glasgow and Highland Royal Mail Steamers'.

In the same year, the first *Iona* was built for the Glasgow to Ardrishaig service, to replace *Mountaineer* after only eight seasons. *Iona* was described as 'The Queen of the Clyde Steamers' by Hugh Macdonald in his book *Days at the Coast*, published in 1857. *Mountaineer* transferred to Oban to run the Staffa and Iona and the Fort William services along with *Pioneer* and, from 1875, was purely on the Oban to Fort William service.

Also in 1855, the paddle steamer *Clansman* was built to replace *Chevalier* on the all-the-way service from Glasgow to Skye. She was wrecked in thick fog off Sanda on 21 July 1869.

In 1857, the Glasgow & Lochfine Steam Packet Company was taken over by Hutchison, along with the three steamers *Mary Jane* (1846), *Inverary Castle* (1839) and *Duke of Argyll* (1852). *Mary Jane* had been built for James Matheson of Stornoway for service from Glasgow to Stornoway and had come into the ownership of the Loch Fyne company in 1851, operating from Glasgow to Inveraray. She was rebuilt in 1875 and renamed *Glencoe*, remaining in service until 1931, when she was withdrawn at the venerable age of eighty-five. After her 1875 rebuild, she operated from Oban to Gairloch, and on the Oban to Fort William and Corpach service. From 1890 to 1905 she was the Islay mail steamer from West Loch Tarbert and her later years, from 1920 onwards, were spent on the Portree mail service from Mallaig and Kyle of Lochalsh.

Inveraray Castle was built for the Glasgow to Inverary service, and spent her whole life on it until being withdrawn in 1889 and scrapped three years later. Her name was altered to *Inverary Castle* in 1862. *Duke of Argyll* sank in the Sound of Mull on 12 January 1858.

Also acquired by Hutcheson in 1857 was the Glasgow & Highland Steam Packet Company and its solitary steamer, *Maid of Lorn* (1849), a slightly larger sister of *Cygnet* and *Lapwing*, which had operated a weekly service from Glasgow to Inverness. She was promptly renamed *Plover* and continued on the same route until sold in 1883, after which her hulk was moored in the Gareloch for a further eight years.

The G. & J. Burns Irish Sea paddle steamer *Stork* was purchased by Hutcheson in 1857, operating in that year from Oban to Portrush, and in the following year from Glasgow to Stornoway, after which she was sold.

In 1861 the first screw steamer in the fleet, *Fingal*, was built. She operated from Glasgow to Stornoway, but was sold for blockade running in the American Civil War after only four months in service. She made one run to Savannah, was trapped there and rebuilt as the ironclad *Atlanta* by the Confederate Navy, later being later captured by the Union Navy and used similarly by them.

The paddle steamer *Fairy* was built for the Caledonian Canal service in 1861, but was too large for the route. After a summer in 1862 on the Staffa and Iona service from Oban and a spell relieving the second *Iona* in autumn 1863, she was sold for blockade running.

The year 1862 saw the building of the screw steamer *Clydesdale* to replace *Fingal* on the Glasgow–Stornoway service. She remained with the company until wrecked in January 1905 on the Lady Rock, off the south end of Lismore.

Iona was sold for blockade running in autumn 1862, but was run down and sunk off Greenock Esplanade on her delivery voyage on 2 October 1862. A successor was built with the same name and similar design, although 24 feet longer and with deck saloons. She too was sold for blockade running after her first season in 1863. Her deck saloons were removed and she set sail for America, but was sunk off Lundy in the Bristol Channel after seeking shelter in a storm on 2 January 1864.

The year 1863 saw the building of a small screw steamer named *Staffa* for the service from Glasgow to Inverness via the Mull of Kintyre, on which she remained until wrecked off the west of Gigha on 23 August 1886.

A third *Iona* was built in 1864, inheriting the deck saloons of her predecessor, and she was to enjoy a long career with the company, remaining in service until 1935.

Three steamers were built in 1866 for portions of the Royal Route, all of which enjoyed remarkable longevity. Paddle steamer *Gondolier* was built for the Caledonian Canal service from Banavie to Inverness, which she served for seventy-four years until the outbreak of war in 1939. Paddle steamer *Chevalier* was built for the Crinan to Oban and Corpach route, which she served until the First World War, remaining in the fleet until being wrecked on Barmore Island in Loch Fyne on 25 March 1927 while seeing winter service on the Glasgow to Ardrishaig service. *Linnet*, a little twin screw steamer described as a 'floating tramcar', operated the link on the Crinan Canal from Ardrishaig to Crinan until 1929, when she was sold for use as a yacht club-house on the Gareloch. She was wrecked in a storm in January 1932.

The paddle steamer *Islay* of 1849 was purchased by Hutcheson in February 1868 and renamed *Dolphin* but saw little service and was sold in July of the same year.

Following the loss of *Clansman* a screw steamer of the same name was built in 1870 for the Glasgow to Stornoway route, where she remained until withdrawn in 1909.

In 1875 the paddle steamer *Islay* (1867), owned by a consortium of Ileachs (Islay inhabitants), which operated from

Glasgow to Portrush and Islay and from West Loch Tarbert to Islay, was purchased by Hutcheson. She remained on the service until wrecked at Red Bay, on the County Antrim Coast, in 1890.

In 1875 Hutcheson purchased the Loch Awe steamer *Queen of the Lake* (1863), which was withdrawn seven years later, and in 1876 they built the new *Lochawe* for the loch. She enabled an alternative to the Royal Route to be offered between Ardrishaig and Oban, with a coach from Ardrishaig to Ford at the foot of the loch, a steamer to the north end of the loch and, until 1880, a coach from the Pass of Brander to Oban and then, from the opening of the Callander & Oban Railway in that year, a train from Loch Awe station to Oban.

The year 1877 saw a new screw steamer, *Lochiel*, which was operated on various routes in the West Highlands and Islands until she ran ashore at Portree in 1907 and was later broken up.

The year 1878 saw the advent of the finest and most magnificent steamer that has ever operated on the Clyde, *Columba*. She was built to operate on the Glasgow to Ardrishaig service in the peak summer months and did so until summer 1935. Her hull was of steel rather than iron, her deck saloons extended to the edge of the hull, unlike those of *Iona*, which were narrow and had alleyways running along each side, and, at 301.4 feet, she was the longest ever Clyde steamer. Patronised in First Class by the aristocracy travelling to their shooting lodges in the Western Isles, she boasted a hairdresser's salon and a Post Office on board.

David Hutcheson had retired in 1876 at the age of seventy-seven and his brother Alexander did the same in 1878. David MacBrayne had been running the company for a number of years and in 1879 the company name was changed to David MacBrayne.

Above left: Dolphin (1844). Few images survive of steamers from the era before photography.

Above right: Glengarry, ex *Edinburgh Castle* (1844), after her 1875 rebuild when the aft saloon was added and the funnel moved forward of the paddle wheels.

Below Right: Pioneer (1844) berthed at Corpach in a colour postcard view from the early 1890s.

Mountaineer (1852) in Oban Bay.

Mountaineer, doing what it says on the tin! Aground at low tide on Lady Rock, south of Lismore, after running aground there on 25 September 1889.

The speedy *Iona* (1855) off Toward, from a lithograph by William Clark.

Above left: Mary Jane in Tarbert inner harbour in 1858, in what is believed to be the earliest photo taken of a Clyde steamer.

Above right: Glencoe off Kyle of Lochalsh in the 1920s, when she was on the Portree mail service.

Below left: Glencoe, ex *Mary Jane*, at West Loch Tarbert in a coloured postcard view taken between 1890 and 1905 when she was on the Islay service.

Below right: Glencoe, then eighty-five years old, berthed alongside the new *Lochfyne* at the Broomielaw when she was on display there on 4 June 1931, during Glasgow Civic Week, a few months before she was sold for scrapping.

Above: Hutcheson's *Fingal* (1861) as the United States Navy ironclad gunboat *Atlanta* between 1864 and 1869.

Right: *Inveraray Castle* (1839) in her later years, after a small deck saloon was added aft.

Clydesdale (1862), following re-boilering in 1893, when a second funnel was added.

The second *Iona*, of 1863, in an engraving from the *Illustrated London News*.

Iona (1864) arriving at Gourock.

"Waverley" and "Iona" at Arrochar Pier.

Above left: Iona at the Broomielaw, showing her narrow deck saloons to advantage. Williamson's *Strathmore* is departing for Rothesay and the Kyles of Bute.

Above right: Iona at Arrochar with the LNER's *Waverley* (1899) during the 1920s.

Below left: Iona arriving at Ardrishaig with *Columba* already berthed there in a coloured postcard view.

Below right: Iona at Fort William in 1935 during her final spell of service, with *Lochfyne* berthed alongside her.

S.S. "Gondolier" in Locks, Fort Augustus.   1775

Gondolier descending the locks at Fort Augustus.

S.S. "CHEVALIER" APPROACHING CRINAN PIER

Chevalier (1866) approaching Crinan.

Linnet in the Crinan Canal after a raised steering platform was fitted to her in 1906.

Clansman (1870) arriving at Stornoway in a tinted postcard view.

Lochawe (right) with *Countess of Breadalbane*, owned by the proprietor of the Lochawe Hotel, at Ford at the south end of the loch.

Islay (1867) at Port Askaig.

Lochiel (1877) at the original pier at West Loch Tarbert. She was on the Islay service from 1879 until 1881.

Above: A three-quarter bow view of *Columba* on the Firth of Clyde.

Right: *Fingal* (1877) in Oban Bay, approaching the Railway Pier.

A stern view of *Columba* departing Dunoon.

Columba and the Inveraray steamer *Lord of the Isles* racing in Loch Fyne in 1910, clearly consuming copious amounts of coal.

Above: Columba at Tarbert Pier.

Top right: A deck view on *Columba* taken from a contemporary illustrated book.

Below left: Columba and *Iona* berthed at Ardrishaig.

Below right: Columba in Govan dry dock being readied for her final season in 1935.

R.M.S. Columba and Iona at Ardrishaig.

Chapter 2

DAVID MACBRAYNE: 1879–1905

David MacBrayne was sixty-five years old when the company started operating under his own name. He carried on running the business until he retired in 1906 at the age of ninety-one. His two sons, David Hope MacBrayne and Laurence MacBrayne, assisted him in the running of the operation and became partners in 1902. When David MacBrayne became a limited company in 1905, David Hope MacBrayne became its chairman.

The 1880s saw a handful of new ships built, and then a succession of second-hand vessels purchased. The early years of the twentieth century saw a tentative dip into the waters of the new technology of the motor ship.

The year 1881 saw the building of *Claymore*, a magnificent screw steamer for the Glasgow to Stornoway route, a service she maintained until 1931. The round trips from Glasgow were sold as what nowadays would be termed mini-cruises, but she was, in the main, a year-round lifeline for the Islands.

Cavalier followed in 1883, a passenger-cargo steamer for the route from Glasgow to Inverness, her size constrained by the dimension of the locks on the Caledonian Canal. She replaced the 1848 *Cygnet*, although now sailing round the Mull of Kintyre rather than through the Crinan Canal. She was sold in 1919 to the North of Scotland, Orkney & Shetland Steam Navigation Co. Ltd and renamed *Fetlar*, although she only saw one year's service there and was then sold to an Irish Sea operator.

The year 1885 saw the paddle steamer *Grenadier* built for the Oban to Gairloch service, but after one season she was moved to the Staffa and Iona route, where she became a firm favourite until her end came on the night of 5 September 1927, when she was gutted by fire while lying at Oban overnight. 1880 had seen the opening of the railway to Oban and the resulting increase in tourists had made the Oban to Staffa and Iona excursion one of the most popular on the West Coast. *Grenadier* was used in the winter months on the Ardrishaig mail service.

The year 1885 saw the purchase of the first of a succession of second-hand steamers, the paddle steamer *Loch Foyle*, which had been built as *Lochgoil* in 1853 for the Glasgow to Lochgoilhead service. She had been sold for use at Londonderry in 1875 and returned to the Clyde in 1877, where she was used as a Sunday breaker. MacBrayne renamed her *Lochness* and used her on the Loch Ness mail servicer from Inverness to Fort Augustus, replacing *Fingal*. She was on this route until scrapped in 1912.

Also purchased in 1885 was *Ethel*, built in 1880 for northern Irish owners. She was placed on the Glasgow to Inverness service alongside *Cavalier*, although purely carrying cargo. In 1910 she was renamed *Clansman* and she was sold in 1916.

The small cargo steamer *Aros Castle* was purchased in 1887 from Martin Orme and renamed *Handa*. She was used in 1888 to operate a new outer islands mail service and then on a variety of cargo services such as that to Loch Sunart. She was small enough to pass through the Crinan Canal and, because of her large cargo-carrying capacity, was known as 'MacBrayne's Gladstone Bag'. She was in service until 1917.

The steam launch *Mabel*, operating on Loch Maree and owned by the manager of the Gairloch Hotel, was purchased in 1887 and remained in service until 1911 before being abandoned on the shore of the loch.

Another 1887 purchase was *Countess of Kellie*, which had been built in 1870 for a cross-river ferry service at Alloa. She had been built as a paddle steamer, but was converted to screw propulsion before entering service for MacBrayne, for whom she

was used for transporting coal for the steamers from Glasgow to the West Coast until sold in 1904.

The final purchase of 1887 was the cargo steamer *Gladiator*, which had been built in 1860 and appears to have been used as a tramp steamer on international voyages. She ran aground off the southern Spanish coast in December 1893 while on a voyage from Mauritius to London.

In 1888 the small coaster *Udea*, built in 1873, was purchased. She was used on the Loch Fyne and other cargo services and was wrecked off Gigha in April 1894.

A second *Staffa* joined the fleet in 1888, built in 1861 for Portuguese owners. She was placed on the Outer Islands mail service and was sold in 1909.

The paddle stammer *Fusilier* was built in 1888 and initially ran from Oban to Gairloch but, after a couple of years, operated on excursion services out of Oban, e.g. to Fort William, moving to the Staffa and Iona service after the demise of *Grenadier* in 1927 until *Lochfyne* was built in 1931. She was sold in 1934 for service on the Forth. *Fusilier* was the final steamer to be built for the company in the nineteenth century, the next being *Lapwing* in 1903.

The large screw steamers *Pelican* and *Falcon* were also purchased in 1888, the former operating from Oban to Iceland for a while in 1889 and the latter being operated on charter to the Mediterranean. They were wrecked in 1895 off Tobermory and abandoned in November 1890 en route from Glasgow to America respectively.

The small steamer *Margaret* was purchased in 1890 and was involved in coal-carrying for the company until sold four years later.

The cargo steamer *Texa* was purchased in 1889. She had been built in 1884 as *James Mutter* for the Islay cargo service and mainly worked on the Loch Fyne cargo service from Glasgow to Ardrishaig until sold in 1917.

Another deep sea ship, *Loanda*, was purchased in 1889 with a cargo of coal and moored in Broadford Bay as a supply point for the MacBrayne steamers during a coal strike, sailing for German and Polish ports to replenish her stocks when necessary. She was laid up in 1895 and scrapped in 1897.

Also purchased in 1889 was the salvage steamer *Recovery*, which was renamed *Flowerdale* and used on the mail service from Oban to the Outer Islands. She was the first twin screw steamer in the fleet, and was lost off Lismore in 1904.

In 1889 the steam launch *Maud* was chartered for use in the summit portion of the Caledonian Canal during a drought which rendered it impassable by the larger steamers. She had been built for T. B. Seath of Rutherglen, for whom she had operated as a steam yacht. She was purchased by MacBrayne later that year and in 1893 was transferred to Loch Shiel to run from a hotel at Shiel Bridge, owned by Mr MacBrayne, where she ran until 1897. She ran mainly fishing trips on Loch Shiel, but made a round trip to Glenfinnan in the summer months, connecting with coaches from Salen, Loch Sunart at the south end and to Fort William and Arisaig at the north end. At 10 tons, she was the smallest vessel in the list of the company's ships in their guidebooks and timetables.

The Clyde paddle steamer *Hero*, built in 1858, was purchased by David MacBrayne in 1890 and initially briefly replaced *Iona*, which was being reboilered, on the Ardrishaig mail service, running from Greenock. In 1892 she was rebuilt with a clipper bow and a deck saloon and renamed *Mountaineer*. She was used on excursions and local services from Oban and was sold for scrapping in 1909.

The Stranraer to Larne paddle steamer *Princess Louise* (1872) was purchased in December 1890 and, renamed *Islay*, was placed on the Glasgow to Islay service, replacing the previous steamer of that name, which had been wrecked earlier that month. She maintained this service until wrecked near Port Ellen in July 1902.

The paddle steamer *Great Western* was purchased from the Great Western Railway in spring 1891 and placed on the Stornoway mail service from Strome Ferry. She was renamed *Lovedale* in 1893 and the mainland terminal changed to Kyle of Lochalsh when the railway opened in 1897. She served until broken up in 1904.

Gael, a paddle steamer that had been built in 1867 for the Campbeltown and Glasgow service and had later operated for the Great Western Railway from Weymouth to the Channel Islands, among other services, was purchased by MacBrayne in 1891. She was placed on the Oban to Portree and Gairloch route, which she maintained until it ceased on the outbreak of war in 1914. After the war she was used on various routes and as a director's yacht, and was scrapped in 1924.

The next purchase was the old paddle steamer *Cygnus* (1854) in December 1890. She had operated from Weymouth to the Channel Islands and was placed on the Loch Fyne cargo service to replace the venerable *Inverary Castle* of 1839. In 1892 she was rebuilt and renamed *Brigadier*, emerging with a single funnel rather than the previous two. She was placed on the Strome Ferry to Portree mail service, and was later on the Oban–Loch

Sunart service and occasionally on the Outer Isles service as a relief steamer. While on this duty, she was wrecked near Rodel, Harris, in December 1896.

In 1893 the paddle steamer *Albert Edward* (1878) was purchased from the joint railway companies (LB&SCR and L&SWR) service from Portsmouth to the Isle of Wight. She was renamed *Carabinier* and operated on the service from Oban to the Sound of Mull, Tobermory and Loch Sunart until sold for breaking up in 1908.

The 1890s brought the regular charter of the steamer *Aggie* on the Loch Fyne cargo service and 1894 the purchase of the steamer *Hibernian*, which was used on deep sea tramping work for a few months until lost off Douglas, Isle of Man, in August 1894.

In late 1894 MacBrayne purchased the veteran Clyde steamer *Ardmore*, ex-*Sultan* (1861), shortened her, adding a canoe type bow, renamed her *Gairlochy* and placed her on the Caledonian Canal service opposite *Gondolier*, which she maintained until destroyed by fire at Fort Augustus on 24 December 1919. She replaced *Glengarry*, which went to the Loch Ness mail service as a second steamer.

The year 1902 saw the entry of the final second-hand steamer into the fleet at this time, with the purchase of the paddle steamer *La Belgique*. She had been built in 1875 for the Newhaven to Dieppe service as *Paris*, and later operated from Liverpool to North Wales, from Hamburg to Helgoland as *Flamingo*, and as an excursion steamer from Tilbury to Ostend for one season only in 1897. MacBrayne renamed her *Glendale* and she operated on a number of routes including the Oban to Gairloch service and the Stornoway mail service. She was on the Glasgow–Islay service when she was wrecked on Deas Point, Kintyre, on 20 July 1905.

The loss of so many steamers by grounding over the years reflects the times before the advent of radar and GPS, when navigation in the treacherous waster of the West Highlands and Islands was in many cases a matter of 'by guess and by God'.

By 1902 the MacBrayne fleet was a veritable museum of ancient steamers, with a fleet of thirty, the average age of which was thirty-two years.

The addition of new blood to the company in 1902, in the form of David MacBrayne's two sons, saw the first newly built steamer for fifteen years built in the following year, *Lapwing*. She was the first of a trio of similar workmanlike screw steamers for year-round operation to the Outer Isles. She commenced operation on the Oban to Outer Islands service and moved to the Portree to Harris and Lochmaddy route in 1908. On 28 January 1917 she ran aground on Rat Rock, Oban, and was sold in the following year to Clyde Cargo Steamers Ltd, for whom she became *Cowal* and sailed until 1931.

Sheila was the second new build of the decade, appearing in 1904 and going on the Stornoway mail service from Kyle of Lochalsh, which she served for most of her life. She was lost on 1 January 1927 when she ran aground near the entrance of Loch Torridon inbound from Stornoway. No lives were lost, however.

Plover was the first of the two quasi-sisters of *Lapwing*, appearing in 1904. She worked to the Outer Isles from Oban, Mallaig (the railway having opened to there in 1901) and Kyle of Lochalsh. In 1934 she was remodelled and became the directors' yacht, being renamed *Loch Aline*. She was sold in 1947 and converted to a cargo steamer. Four years later she was scrapped.

Cygnet was the third of the trio, and differed from her two sisters in having little passenger accommodation and no berths. She was initially on the Glasgow to Inveraray cargo service, relieving her sisters on the Outer Isles services for their overhauls. After the First World War she was on the Inner Islands services from Oban, on basically a similar run to that which was in force until comparatively recently from Oban to Coll, Tiree, Castlebay, Barra and Lochboisdale, South Uist. She was fitted with sleeping berths for this service, but she was not popular with the paying public, who regarded her as a cargo steamer doing as passenger run. She was sold for breaking up in September 1930, having been replaced by the new motorships *Lochmor* and *Lochearn*.

Brenda was another cargo steamer built in 1904. She was small enough to pass through the Crinan Canal, and operated initially from Glasgow to Inverness and latterly only as far as Fort William. She was sold for scrapping in 1929.

The penultimate paddle steamer built for MacBrayne, *Pioneer*, came in 1905 for the West Loch Tarbert to Islay route, which she served on all her life. In 1944 she was requisitioned by the Admiralty, and was later purchased by them and served under the name HMS *Harbinger* on anti-submarine warfare duties. In 1946 her engines and paddle wheels were removed and she was taken to Portland, where she served as a floating laboratory until broken up in 1958.

The final steamer to be built prior to the formation of the limited company was the *Clydesdale* of 1905, built for the Glasgow to Inverness cargo and passenger service. A few weeks after she came out *Glendale* was lost and she moved to the Glasgow to Islay route. After the loss of *Sheila* in 1927 she moved to the Stornoway mail service until *Lochness* entered service in 1929. She operated on a number of other West Coast routes until she was scrapped in 1953.

In December 1905 Laurence MacBrayne sold his 25 per cent share in the company to his brother David Hope MacBrayne, and on 1 January 1906 David MacBrayne Ltd was incorporated. At this time David MacBrayne retired at the age of ninety-one, although he still went in to the office every day. He died on 26 January 1907 at the age of ninety-two.

S.S. "Claymore" at Gairloch Pier

Claymore (1881) at Flowerdale Pier, Gairloch, in a tinted postcard view posted in 1908.

A stern view of *Claymore*.

S.S. CLAYMORE AT OBAN.

Above: Claymore in Oban Bay.

Right: The figurehead from the 1881 *Claymore*, now an exhibit in the Scottish Maritime Museum in Irvine.

Below: Claymore in the grey livery carried for a short period in 1929.

Above left: The Glasgow to Inverness steamer *Cavalier* (1883) descending Neptune's Staircase at Banavie.

Above right: *Cavalier* arriving at Ballachulish Pier.

Below right: The Staffa and Iona paddle steamer *Grenadier* (1885) in Oban Bay.

Below left: *Grenadier* moored off Iona in her original condition with thin funnels prior to her 1902–3 re-boilering.

Above left: *Grenadier* landing passengers at Staffa in a postcard view from the Royal Route series.

Above right: *Grenadier* off Staffa in the 1920s.

Below left: *Grenadier* as the minesweeper HMS *Grenade* during the First World War.

Below right: The sunken *Grenadier* after her fatal fire at Oban on 5 September 1927.

The Pier, Invermorriston

The veteran *Lochness*, ex *Lough Foyle*, ex *Lochgoil*, approaching Invermoriston Pier on Loch Ness.

The cargo steamer *Handa*, 'MacBrayne's Gladstone Bag', departing Blackmillbay pier on Luing.

Above: The coal lighter *Countess of Kellie* moored outside *Cavalier* in Glasgow with the paddle tug *Fairweather* in mid-stream and *Clutha No. 12* and another unidentified *Clutha* on the far side of the river.

Left: The steam launch *Mabel* on Loch Maree.

The cargo steamer *Udea* at Ardrishaig, seen to the left of the pier, with *Iona* berthed to the right.

Staffa (1861), which was in the fleet from 1888 to 1909, serving on the Outer Islands mail service.

Fusilier (1888) arriving at Ardgour in Loch Linnhe.

Ballachulish Pier and S.S. "Fusilier."

Fusilier at Ballachulish Pier.

The deep-sea cargo steamer *Pelican* (1850), built for the City of Cork Steam Packet Co. and purchased by MacBrayne in 1888 for a short-lived new service from Oban to Iceland.

Falcon (1854), with a similar story to *Pelican*. Both appear to have been used in the deep sea tramping trade by MacBrayne.

The cargo steamer *Texa* on the Clyde off Erskine.

Flowerdale at Oban Railway pier.

Mountaineer, ex *Hero* (1857), after
being rebuilt with a clipper bow in
1892, approaching Onich pier at the
entrance to Loch Leven.

Above: Islay, ex *Princess Louise* (1872), at Port Askaig.

Left: Islay after she ran aground on Sheep Island, Port Ellen, on 15 July 1902 in dense fog.

Lovedale (1867) berthed at Kyle of Lochalsh.

Gael (1867) arriving at Portree in a coloured postcard view.

Gael off Dunoon in 1919, while on charter to the Caledonian Steam Packet Co., replacing steamers that were still reconditioning after their war service. Note the crowd of passengers on her promenade deck.

Brigadier, ex *Cygnus* (1854).

Above: Caledonian Canal steamer *Glengarry*, ex *Sultan* (1861), in the Caledonian Canal.

Right: The former Portsmouth to Ryde steamer *Albert Edward* (1878), now MacBrayne's *Carabinier*.

Glendale (1875) arriving at Tobermory with *Claymore* in the background.

Glendale aground off the Mull of Kintyre, 20 July 1905.

Lapwing (1902) in the River Clyde, passing a Laird Line steamer.

The Stornoway mail steamer *Sheila* (1904) at Kyle of Lochalsh. Note the railway wagon on the pier.

Left: Plover (1904), sitting on the bottom at Balmacara for bottom cleaning and painting.

Below: Loch Aline, ex *Plover,* at Ardrossan.

Cygnet at Oban (Railway Pier) in a postcard view.

The cargo steamer *Brenda* (1904) off Fort William.

Pioneer (1905), the penultimate paddle steamer to be built for MacBrayne, arriving at Port Askaig with the Paps of Jura in the background.

Top left: *Pioneer* off Port Askaig with a large crowd of passengers on board.

Top right: *Clydesdale* (1905) at Oban.

Bottom left: *Pioneer* at West Loch Tarbert pier, with a long queue of passengers.

Bottom right: Anti-submarine warfare vessel HMS *Harbinger*, ex *Pioneer*.

Chapter 3

DAVID MACBRAYNE LTD: 1906–28

In 1906 the first motor bus service operated by MacBrayne, from Fort William to North Ballachulish, commenced. Competition from bus services would lead to the demise of many steamer services and pier calls over the ensuing decades, while MacBrayne would operate an increasing network of bus services in the area until 1972.

The first new vessel for the new limited company was the small motor vessel *Comet*, purchased in 1907. She had been used on the Thames under the name of *Win* for two years, probably as a private yacht. She was used on a new service from Ballachulish to Kinlochleven. Kinlochleven at that time was a hub of industry, with the construction of an aluminium smelting plant, and of dams in the hills above it to provide hydro-electric power for the smelter. After the First World War she moved to the Clyde, and after a season operating from Ardrishaig to Inveraray in connection with *Columba* in 1919, operated the Greenock–Lochgoilhead mail service until October 1946. In 1947 she was sold to owners at Shoreham, West Sussex, and after a short spell operating from there, was converted for use as a houseboat, a state in which she remains today. She is one of only a handful of surviving MacBrayne vessels.

A second small motor vessel for the Loch Leven service, *Scout*, was built in 1907. She was destroyed by fire on 19 August 1913 after an engine blowback. Both these early motor vessels used paraffin for fuel.

Also in 1907, the magnificent steamer *Chieftain* was built to replace *Clansman* (1870) on the Glasgow to Stornoway service. She was rather large and fuel-hungry for the service, and was sold in 1919 to the North of Scotland, Orkney & Shetland Steam Navigation Co. Ltd, who renamed her *St Margaret*. In 1925 she was sold by them to Canadian National Steamship Co. Ltd and renamed *Prince Charles*, being sold again and used for the Israeli emigrant trade before being broken up in 1952.

A third paraffin-engined motor vessel, *Lochinvar*, was built in 1908 for the Oban to Tobermory mail service to replace *Carabinier*. Her appearance altered over the years, starting with a tall, thin funnel, progressing to three bare exhaust pipes, one for each engine, and finally to a squat 'motorship'-type funnel. In 1959 she was transferred to the Portree mail service, but was not a success there, and was withdrawn that October. She was sold in the following spring for use on the Medway under the name *Anzio I*. In spring 1966 she was sold for a new route from Inverness to Invergordon, but was wrecked near the mouth of the Humber on her delivery voyage with the loss of all hands.

A second *Lochiel* was built in 1908 to replace *Lapwing* on the Inner Islands service from Oban. She was requisitioned by the Admiralty in January 1917 and was sunk by a U-boat off Whitby on 24 July 1918 while acting as an escort vessel, with the loss of twelve lives.

Nellie was a cargo steamer dating from 1892, which had been on charter to the company and was purchased in 1908, being renamed *Staffa* in 1910. She operated the cargo service from Glasgow to Mull and Loch Leven via the Crinan Canal alongside *Brenda* and was sold in 1916.

Dirk was a smaller steamer built in 1909. She was based at Tobermory and ran the mail service to Coll, Tiree, and Bunessan. She was sunk by a German U-boat on 28 May 1918 off Flamborough Head while on war service as a patrol boat.

The company's final paddle steamer, *Mountaineer*, was built in 1910. She was similar to *Pioneer* but did not have the promenade deck carried forward to the bow. She was used on routes out of Oban, often on the Fort William service, and also in peak season to assist *Pioneer* on the Islay service.

In 1911 the Loch Leven Shipping Company Ltd was purchased along with the motor launch *Cona* and the small steamer *Loch Leven Queen*. These operated on the Ballachulish to Kinlochleven service, *Cona* sometimes towing rowing boats for extra passengers. *Loch Leven Queen* had begun life as *Clutha No. 12* on the Clyde in 1896. In 1912 she was renamed *Lochness* and placed on the Loch Ness mail service in succession to the paddle steamer of the same name. She was sold for scrapping in 1929. The Kinlochleven service ceased in 1923 and was replaced by road transport.

In 1912 the goodwill of the Lochgoilhead mail service of the Lochgoil & Inveraray Steamboat Co. Ltd was purchased. Initially operated by *Chevalier* and *Mountaineer*, *Comet* was moved there in 1914.

The two paddle stammers *Edinburgh Castle* (1879) and *Lord of the Isles* (1891) were purchased by Turbine Steamers Ltd. The former was sold for breaking up in 1913. The latter continued in service on excursions until 1928, being chartered by David MacBrayne Ltd to replace *Iona* on the Lochgoilhead and Arrochar routes in her final season.

Two small screw steamers were purchased in 1914 to replace *Scout* on the Kinlochleven route, *Countess of Mayo* (1897), which originally operated on the River Shannon in Ireland, and *Duke of Abercorn* (1888), which had boiler problems and was scrapped in the following year.

Unlike the main Clyde operators, only one MacBrayne paddle steamer was taken over by the Admiralty in the First World War, *Grenadier*, which served as the minesweeper HMS *Grenade* from 1916 to 1919. The screw steamers *Dirk* and *Lochiel*, as mentioned above, were both requisitioned by the Admiralty in 1917, and both were sunk by U-boats in the following year. The paucity of remaining steamers on the railway companies' Clyde services led to a number of MacBrayne vessels being chartered for service on the Clyde between 1916 and 1919. The paddle steamers *Chevalier*, *Fusilier*, *Gael*, *Glencoe* and *Mountaineer* and the motor vessel *Lochinvar* were thus employed. The drop in tourist numbers during the war years meant that most of these steamers would otherwise have been laid up due to lack of custom.

A steamer named *Devonia*, which had operated from Plymouth to Brittany, was purchased in 1919 to replace the war loss *Lochiel*. She was renamed *Lochiel*, and operated on the Glasgow to Stornoway cargo service and other cargo services until 1937, being sold in the following year.

The motor lighter *C & B No. 1* (1913), originally owned by Crosse & Blackwell, was purchased in 1928 for use in transhipment of cargos at Bowmore in Islay. She was renamed *Lochgorm* in 1930 and *Iona* in 1936 and was withdrawn in 1937 when replaced by road transport.

The loss of three steamers in 1927, *Sheila*, *Chevalier* and *Grenadier*, dealt a body blow to the company, now with an aging fleet and seeing many of its services hit by road competition, and in 1928 the company refused to tender for the mail contract. After considerable debate in Parliament a lifeline was offered by Sir Alfred Read, Chairman of the Coast Lines Group, and Sir Josiah Stamp, President of the London, Midland & Scottish Railway. These two companies jointly took over the fleet and goodwill of David MacBrayne Ltd, forming a new company called David MacBrayne (1928) Ltd on 1 November 1928 to continue operations.

MacBrayne's first motor vessel, *Comet* (1905).

Comet in her present guise, as a houseboat at Shoreham by Sea.

Scout (1907) berthed at Ballachulish among the piles of slate waste.

Scout after the fire which destroyed her on 19 August 1913.

The magnificent, clipper-bowed *Chieftain*.

Above left: Lochinvar (1908) in her original condition with a tall funnel.

Above right: Lochinvar arriving at Mallaig, when on the Portree mail service in 1959, her final season.

Below left: Lochinvar in later condition with three exhaust pipes, one for each engine in place of a funnel, at Oban.

Below right: Lochinvar after 1933 with a single funnel, arriving at Oban. Note the two cars as deck cargo forward of the funnel below the crane.

Mountaineer after the solid bulwarks were replaced by conventional rails around 1926.

Mountaineer arriving at Crinan in her final month in service, September 1938.

Lochness, ex *Loch Leven Queen*, ex *Clutha No. 12*, at Inverness.

The Bowmore lighter *C & B No. 1 c.* 1929, prior to being renamed *Lochgorm*.

Chapter 4

DAVID MACBRAYNE (1928) LTD AND DAVID MACBRAYNE LTD: 1928–47

The new company came into being on 1 November 1928, with the proviso that at least four new ships were built in the following two years.

One advantage of the new ownership was that ships could be transferred from other companies in the Coast Lines group. The first purchase of the new company was *Denbigh Coast* from Coast Lines Ltd in May 1929. She had been built in 1891 for G. & J. Burns as *Grouse*, being sold to Grahamston Shipping Ltd in 1922 and renamed *Kelvindale*, and then to Coast Lines in 1924. She was renamed *Lochdunvegan*, and placed on the Glasgow to Stornoway and other cargo services. She was sold for scrapping in 1948.

In July 1929, the first new-built ship of the new era entered service, *Lochness*, to replace *Sheila* on the Stornoway mail service. Somewhat anachronistically, she had reciprocating steam machinery, with two triple expansion engines driving twin

screws. She served Stornoway faithfully in calm and storm, in peace and war, until replaced by *Loch Seaforth* in 1947. She was then used on the Inner Isles service from Oban while *Lochearn* was being re-engined, and then as spare steamer, until sold to Italian owners in 1955. Sold on again to Greek owners in 1958, she remained in service until broken up in 1973.

The cargo vessel *Lochshiel* was built in 1929 to replace *Brenda* on the Glasgow to Mull and Loch Sunart service. She was a motor vessel and introduced the engines-aft motor cargo vessel design to the fleet, a type which remained until the car ferry era.

The year 1930 saw two sister ships, *Lochearn* and *Lochmor*, modern motorships with good passenger accommodation, being built for the Inner Isles service from Oban to Lochboisdale and for the Outer Isles service, which ran from Kyle of Lochalsh to Scalpay, Tarbert (Harris), Rodel, Lochmaddy, and Lochboisdale, returning to Mallaig via the Small Isles of Canna, Eigg and Rhum. This circuit was undertaken twice weekly in each direction in the peak summer months and thrice weekly in the remainder of the year. Before the war, calls were also made once weekly at Stockinish in Harris and, in the winter months, at Dunvegan between Lochmaddy and Lochboisdale, and at Armadale and Glenelg when the thrice weekly schedule meant that each trip was a full circle, rather than reversing the itinerary at Mallaig. *Lochearn* spent most her career on the Inner Isles service until she was replaced by *Claymore* in 1955, when she went onto the Sound of Mull mail service. *Lochmor* was on the Outer Isles service until replaced by the car ferries in 1964. In 1964 both were used on the car ferry routes for a few months until the car ferries could be delivered, *Lochearn* on Oban to Craignure and Lochaline and *Lochmor* from Mallaig to Armadale. In August 1964 both were sold to Greek owners but saw no service, as far as is known, in Greek waters, and both were scrapped a few years later.

The period from 1929 to 1930 saw a brief foray into grey hulls with *Lochness*, *Lochearn* and *Lochmor* originally sporting them and *Clansman* and *Columba* being painted in this way, although that on *Columba* only lasted a fortnight. Public reaction was not favourable and the experiment was soon dropped.

In 1931, the sixty-year-old steamer *City of London* was purchased from the Aberdeen Steam Navigation Co., and renamed *Lochbroom* for the service from Glasgow to the west coast. She terminated at Lochinver, in place of the old *Claymore*, ten years her junior, although she did not normally serve Stornoway. A 1934 timetable shows her sailing from Glasgow every ten days between May and October for Greenock, Oban, Tobermory, Eigg, Mallaig, Kyle of Lochalsh, Portree, Gairloch, Ullapool and Lochinver, extended to Lochinchard (Loch Clash pier) on certain sailings. The cost of the cruise was £10 in a two-berth stateroom, with a 20 per cent reduction on sailings up to and including 20 May and from and including 23 September. With sleeping berths for over eighty passengers, she certainly needed the income from cruise traffic. She was sold for breaking up in July 1937.

Lochfyne, the fourth of the ships to be built under the 1928 agreement, was revolutionary, being the first British passenger vessel to be powered by diesel-electric machinery. This, although an advance on the old paddle steamers, produced major noise and vibration. She was instantly recognisable by her two widely-spaced funnels. She indirectly replaced *Gondolier* on the Staffa and Iona sailings from Oban in the summer months, and relieved *Columba* on the Ardrishaig mail service in the winter months. In 1936, when *King George V* took over the Staffa and Iona service, she was moved to the Oban to Fort William service in the summer months. During the Second World War she was on the Ardrishaig run year-round, sailing from Wemyss Bay because of the boom across the Clyde south of Dunoon. In 1946 she was back on the Staffa and Iona and Fort William services from Oban, and from 1947 until 1958 she was employed in the summer months on cruises from Oban, including the popular Six Lochs cruise, as well as the Fort William service. In summer 1959 she replaced *Saint Columba* and was on the Ardrishaig mail service year round, although this only ran as far as Tarbert in the winter months, and had not run from Glasgow since 1939. She was withdrawn after the 1969 summer season and was then sold, spending some time at Faslane on the Gareloch providing electric power for the shipbreaking yard there. She was scrapped at Dalmuir in 1974.

The early 1930s saw the building of a number of ferry boats for the company, for use at the calls that did not have piers, mainly motor powered, although a couple in use at Rodel and Stockinish on Harris were large rowing boats.

In 1934 the small excursion steamer *Princess Louise*, owned by Alexander Paterson, was purchased by MacBrayne. She had been built in 1898 and operated on short trips out of Oban. From 1935 to 1939 she was used on cruises on Loch Ness from Inverness, and was also on livestock runs. After a spell laid up she was sold in 1939, and was lost while in dry dock in Greenock during an air raid in 1941.

The year 1934 saw the advent of *Lochnevis*, a smaller version of *Lochfyne* with a single funnel. Design changes meant that vibration was kept to a minimum. She indirectly replaced the venerable *Glencoe* on the Mallaig and Kyle to Portree mail service and also offered excursions from Mallaig to Loch Scavaig and from Portree to Gairloch and Loch Torridon. She was on the Wemyss Bay to Tarbert service in early 1940 and was taken up for war service in December 1940 and was used as a minclayer. On the cessation of hostilities she returned to the Portree mail service and from 1959 was based at Oban, replacing *Lochfyne* there. In 1965 she was on the Islay mail service and continued in that on weekends until her withdrawal from service in 1969, sailing out of Oban during the week. She was sold to Holland in 1970 and was broken up there four years later.

In July 1934 the name of the company was changed back to David MacBrayne Ltd.

In October 1935, when Williamson-Buchanan Steamers Ltd was sold to the London, Midland & Scottish Railway, the two steamers of Turbine Steamers Ltd, *Queen Alexandra* and *King George V*, came under the ownership of David MacBrayne Ltd.

Queen Alexandra had been built in 1912 and was rebuilt prior to the 1936 season, for which she emerged with a third funnel. She replaced *Columba* on the Glasgow to Ardrishaig service each summer. From 1940 she was in use as an accommodation ship in East India Harbour, Greenock, for boom defence personnel. It was 1947 before she returned to service on the Ardrishaig service, now sailing from Gourock and berthing overnight at Greenock. She was taken out of service after the 1958 season and was scrapped at Port Glasgow.

King George V was little altered, and was on the Staffa and Iona service from Oban from 1936 until 1939. She saw war service as a tender on the Firth of Clyde, and was present at the Dunkirk evacuation in 1940, where she made five trips and rescued a total of 4,263 troops. 1946 saw her on the Ardrishaig service, prior to a return to the Staffa and Iona service, now sailing from Fort William on one day per week. This she maintained until 1974. In May 1970 she was chartered by the Highlands and Islands Development Board for a week's sailings from Kyle of Lochalsh, Aultbea and Ullapool and in 1971 relieved *Queen Mary II* on the Clyde in the spring, while the Clyde turbine was held up while refitting due to a shipyard strike. She was sold in 1975 for a proposed conversion to a floating restaurant, but languished in dry dock at Cardiff until gutted by fire in August 1981, following which she was scrapped.

In 1937 the steamer *Lairdspool* was transferred from Burns & Laird Lines and was renamed *Lochgorm* for the Glasgow to

Stornoway service. She had been built in 1898 as *Lily* for Laird Line. Passengers ceased to be carried after the outbreak of the Second World War in 1939 and from 1942 to 1945 she was allocated by the Ministry of War Transport to replace McCallum Orme's *Hebrides* from Glasgow to Oban, Coll, Tiree, etc. She was sold for breaking up in 1951.

Also in 1937, the steamer *Lairdsrock* was transferred from Burns & Laird Lines and was renamed *Lochgarry*. She had been built as *Vulture* in 1898 for G. & J. Burns. *Lochgarry* was used in the cruises from Glasgow to the north-west coast, replacing *Lochbroom*. She was requisitioned in 1940, rescuing 1,001 troops on a single voyage from Dunkirk to Dover, and was then engaged as a transport from Scotland to Iceland. She ran aground in a storm off Torr Head, County Antrim, on 21 February 1942 with the loss of at least twenty-three of her crew.

The small launch *Garry* was purchased in 1937 and ran short cruises at Fort William as well as tendering cruise ships calling there. She was used at Glenelg from 1948 and at Rodel until calls ceased at the latter in 1963.

The Dutch-built passenger launch *Lochbuie* was built in 1938 and used for cruises from Fort William to the head of Loch Eil, Loch Corrie and Ballachulish and Kinlochleven. In 1939 she was based at Oban and was requisitioned in September 1939 and used as a hospital launch. She was sold in 1947 for use in the Channel Islands and became a yacht in 1950.

Lochiel was similar to *Lochnevis*, despite having conventional diesel engines, and was built in 1939 to replace *Pioneer* on the Islay service. Due to the need for dredging at West Loch Tarbert pier, she was unable to take up the service immediately on delivery and spent the summer running out of Oban, mainly to Fort William, then had a spell on the Portree mail run from October 1939 to May 1940. She then spent the remainder of her career on the West Loch Tarbert to Islay service, which was extended to include Colonsay from 1949. On 8 October 1960 she sank after striking a submerged rock in West Loch Tarbert and did not resume service following repairs until the following March. She was replaced by the car ferry *Arran* in January 1970 and was sold for use from Fleetwood to the Isle of Man, renamed *Norwest Laird*. That was not a success and she was laid up. In 1974 she was sold for use as a floating restaurant at Bristol under her original name. She remained there until scrapped in 1995.

The Second World War saw the end of the Caledonian Canal service, with *Gondolier*, by then the last steamer operating on the route, being stripped of her engines, paddles, etc., and used as a blockship in Scapa Flow. The fate of various ships requisitioned by the Admiralty has already been mentioned.

The cargo steamer *Ulster Star* was chartered almost continually from 1940 onwards and was painted in MacBrayne colours from 1945 onwards. She continued on charter until sold for scrap in 1949. She had been built in 1904 as *James Crombie* for the Aberdeen, Leith & Moray Firth Shipping Co. Ltd and was an inter-group transfer from the Belfast Steamship Co.

The screw passenger steamer *Robina* was on charter from Coast Lines Ltd from June 1946 until spring 1948, being used in summer 1946 on Oban excursions, and in 1947 on the Gourock to Lochgoilhead service. She had been built in 1914 for use as an excursion steamer out of Morecambe, and operated as such out of Belfast from 1925 until 1939. She was moved to the Channel Islands in 1948, and was purchased by the Southampton, Isle of

Wight & South of England Royal Mail Steam Packet Co. Ltd in August 1948, and was sold for breaking up in 1955. From 1948 onwards, Lochgoilhead and Carrick Castle were served by a MacBrayne bus service connecting with the Glasgow to Inveraray buses at Rest and be Thankful.

December 1947 saw the advent of a new vessel for the Stornoway mail service, *Loch Seaforth*. She replaced *Lochness* and maintained the service until May 1972, when she was replaced by the car ferry *Clansman* and moved to the Inner Islands service from Oban in place of *Claymore*. On 22 March 1973 she ran aground in the Gunna Sound between Tiree and Coll. She was refloated and towed to Tiree, where she sank alongside the pier, blocking access to the pier until May, when a floating crane lifted her and she was towed to Troon for breaking up.

The hospital launch *Galen*, built in 1941, was purchased in 1947 for a new Oban to Lismore service under the name *Lochnell*. She was on the Kyle of Lochalsh to Toscaig run from 1965 until 1968, and then on the Tobermory to Mingary service until sold in 1981. She has since mainly been used as a private yacht on the Clyde, was moved to Shepperton on the Thames in November 2009 for use as a houseboat, and was towed to Faversham and taken out of the water for restoration in 2011. In July 2012 she was offered for sale on eBay but there were no bidders.

The Stornoway cargo steamer *Lochdunvegan* (1891) was the first purchase of the new regime, and introduced the Loch... series of names, which was adhered to for the next thirty-two years, almost without exception.

The cargo motor vessel *Lochshiel* (1929) at Anderston Quay, Glasgow, with Burns Laird's *Lairdshill* astern of her and *Aranmore* on the south side of the river.

Lochness (1929) at Oban in the twilight of her MacBrayne career.

Above: Lochness in 1929, still with a grey hull.

Left: Lochness approaching Tobermory.

Lochearn (1930) off Oban with the cargo door open ready to discharge cargo.

Lochearn heading into a storm in her early years.

The launch of *Lochmor* at Ardrossan Dockyard on 15 May 1930.

Lochmor at Kyle of Lochalsh.

Lochbroom (1871) at Tobermory.

SUNSET AT MALLAIG.   218608.J.V.

A sunset view of *Lochbroom* off Mallaig.

Lochfyne (1931) at Gourock in the 1960s.

Lochfyne, homeward-bound from Ardrishaig, pauses at Dunoon in July 1968.

Above left: *Lochfyne* anchored off Staffa in a postcard view from early in her career, still with the 1931 grey hull.

Above right: Passengers are rowed ashore from *Lochfyne* at Iona, in her grey-hulled condition.

Below left: *Lochfyne* off Fingal's Cave in a postcard from the same series.

Below right: Sheep being loaded onto *Lochfyne* at Croggan Pier, at the entrance to Loch Spelve, Mull, in the mid-1950s.

Above: Patterson's *Princess Louise* (1898) at Dunstaffnage Pier. She ran a regular service to here and Connel from Oban prior to the First World War.

Right: A deck view on *Princess Louise*.

Lochnevis (1934), with *Lochfyne* berthed forward of her, at the so-called Bristol Berth, their overnight resting-place at Greenock.

Lochnevis in West Loch Tarbert.

Above left: Lochnevis.

Above right: A stern view of *Lochnevis*.

Below right: *Lochnevis*, *Lochbroom* and a puffer berthed at Tobermory, with the Mingary ferry *Applecross* berthed across the end of the pier.

TURBINE STEAMER, "SAINT COLUMBA"

A. 3770.

Above: Saint Columba (1912) approaching Gourock in pre-war days with an open bridge, in a Valentine's postcard view.

Left: Saint Columba in Rothesay Bay in her penultimate season, 1957.

Above left: *Saint Columba* arriving at Tarbert in the 1950s.

Above right: *Saint Columba* at speed in the Kyles of Bute in post-war condition.

Below right: The five-funnelled steamer! *Saint Columba* lying in front of *King George V* in the East India Harbour, Greenock.

T.S.S. KING GEORGE V · A4259

Above left: King George V (1926) off Kerrera in pre-war condition, with the Hutcheson monument visible on the hilltop.

Above right: King George V lying alongside Duchess of Hamilton at Gourock in wartime colours.

Below left: King George V off Oban with Lochfyne at the North Pier in a postcard view from 1947.

Below right: King George V departs from Glasgow (Bridge Wharf) on a charter sailing on 2 June 1956.

STEAMER ARRIVING AT RAILWAY PIER, OBAN.

King George V berthed at Fort William in 1971.

King George V at Tobermory in 1972, with *Lochnell* lying across the end of the pier in the foreground.

King George V lying off Iona with the 'wee red boat' *Ulva* (1956) bringing passengers ashore.

Above: The builder's plate and ship's bell of *King George V*, on the promenade deck below the bridge.

Right: The war record plaque displayed on *King George V*.

S.S. "Lochgarry" AT Kyle

Top left: The 1937 acquisition *Lochgorm* (1896) in the Kingston Dock, Glasgow.

Top right: *Lochgarry* off Kyle.

Bottom left: The cruise vessel *Lochgarry* (1898), ex *Vulture*.

The Dutch-built 'seas-coach' *Lochbuie* (19338) lying at anchor off Fort William.

Lochiel (1939) departing from Oban.

The chartered cargo steamer *Ulster Star* (1904).

Robina (1914) during her short spell on charter to
MacBrayne, seen off Gourock in 1947.

Loch Seaforth (1947) arriving at Mallaig.

Lochnell (1941) in original condition.

Chapter 5

DAVID MACBRAYNE LTD: 1948–73

On 1 January 1948 the railways were nationalised, and the 50 per cent share in David MacBrayne Ltd held by the London, Midland & Scottish Railway passed to British Railways.

On the same date the friendly rivals McCallum Orme & Co. Ltd, with their three steamers, were purchased by MacBrayne. This had been a 1929 amalgamation of John McCallum & Co. and Martin Orme & Co. They operated cargo-passenger sailings to the parts of the Hebrides not reached by MacBrayne services, Colonsay, Iona, Coll, Tiree, the Uists, Harris and the west of Skye.

These steamers were *Hebrides*, *Dunara Castle* and *Challenger*. *Hebrides* had been built in 1898 for McCallum. She continued in service until 1952 and was laid up at Gourock when replaced by *Loch Ard*. She was sold for scrapping in 1955.

Dunara Castle was built as far back as 1875 for Martin Orme. She had regularly offered summer trips as cruises to St Kilda or Loch Roag in the west side of Lewis and had evacuated the last inhabitants from St Kilda in 1930. She sailed for MacBrayne's for less than a month and was sold for scrapping in summer 1948.

Challenger (1897) was a small cargo steamer from the fleet of Jack Bros, which had been taken over by McCallum Orme in 1935. She was withdrawn at the end of 1948 and was sold for scrap.

A passenger service was introduced by MacBrayne to Colonsay, previously in the realm of McCallum Orme, from 1948, initially running from Oban by *Lochness*, and from 1949 by *Lochiel* extending her Port Askaig service.

The cargo vessel *Empire Maysong* was purchased in 1948 for the Glasgow to Stornoway service, for which she was renamed *Lochbroom*. She remained in the fleet until sold in 1971.

A second *Lochbuie*, a former RAF air-sea rescue launch, was purchased in 1949 for a new service from Tobermory to

Mingary. She was in service until 1968, when it was found that her hull was extensively affected by rot. The engine was removed and she was scrapped and burnt.

The Canadian-built cargo steamer *Marleen* was purchased from Dutch owners in 1949 and renamed *Loch Frisa*. She operated from Glasgow to the west side of Skye and was sold to Greek owners in 1963. She was the final steam-powered vessel to be purchased by the company.

Two further additions joined the cargo vessel fleet in 1950 and 1951, both engines-aft motor vessels. The Swedish *Örnen* was renamed *Lochdunvegan* and replaced *Lochgorm* on the Glasgow to Stornoway service. She was sold to Greek owners in 1973.

Loch Carron was built for the company in 1951 and served in the Outer Islands service from Glasgow. She made the final MacBrayne cargo sailing from Glasgow, on 28 October 1976. In the following year she was sold to Cypriot owners. Sometime in the 1980s she was reported as having sunk.

In 1953–4 two new vessels were built for service on Loch Shiel, *Rosalind*, soon renamed *Lochshiel*, and *Lochailort*. The Loch Shiel service replaced that of the Loch Shiel Steamboat Co. *Lochshiel* was removed from the loch in 1962 and was then used at Iona until sunk in the Clyde off Toward in 1970 while proceeding to the Gareloch for overhaul. *Lochailort* remained on the loch until sailings ceased there in 1967. 1968 saw her on the Kyle to Toscaig run, but in the following year, after her timbers were found to be in poor condition, she was burnt at Kyle of Lochalsh.

In 1955 the only major passenger vessel to be built between *Loch Seaforth* and the car ferries, *Claymore*, was built for the Inner Islands mail service from Oban. She also, in her early years, operated a car-carrying sailing on a Saturday afternoon from Oban to Salen, Mull. She was sold in 1976 and had a major rebuild for service as a day cruise vessel in Greek waters, emerging as *City of Hydra* and operating from Palaeon Phaleron, near Piraeus to the Saronic Islands until laid up in 1993. She spent several years in lay-up until she sank at her moorings in 2000.

A final cargo vessel, *Loch Ard*, was built in 1955, to replace *Hebrides* on the Outer Islands cargo service from Glasgow. She was moved to the Glasgow to Islay route in 1964, and was withdrawn when the car ferry *Arran* entered service from West Loch Tarbert to Islay in autumn 1969. She was sold to Greek owners in 1971 and sank in the Mediterranean on 7 May 1984.

The motor fishing vessel *Loch Toscaig* was purchased in 1955 for a new service from Kyle of Lochalsh to Toscaig, which replaced the call off Applecross by the Stornoway mail steamer. She was rebuilt with a cargo hold taking the place of the fish hold and was also used on short cruises from Kyle of Lochalsh. In 1964 she was transferred to the Oban to Lismore service and was sold in late 1975.

Loch Arkaig was a wooden-hulled inshore minesweeper purchased in 1959 and converted for passenger operation. She was initially on the Portree mail service from Mallaig and Kyle, and was moved to the Small Isles service from Mallaig in 1964, a service instituted on the withdrawal of the Outer Islands mail service, operated by *Lochmor*, on the advent of the car ferries. From 1965 she was on a combined Small Isles and Portree roster, which she maintained until 1975, when she was purely on the

Small Isles run, with additional Mallaig to Kyle of Lochalsh runs in the summer months. On occasion, she would carry a solitary car for Raasay, perched on the top of her wheelhouse. On 28 March 1979 she sank in Mallaig harbour, and was sold in October of that year.

Loch Eynort was the former Irish pilot boat *Valonia*, purchased in 1961 for the Kyle of Lochalsh to Portree service, which she operated until 1964. She was then laid up in the Gareloch, seeing little service until sold in 1971 for use as a yacht.

The launch *Highlander* was purchased in 1963, and was renamed *Applecross* for the Kyle to Toscaig service. In the following year she was briefly on the Tobermory to Mingary route and was then moved to Iona, where she remained until sold in 1969 to a Mr Gibson for the Fionnphort to Iona service. In 1973 that service was taken over by Caledonian MacBrayne and she returned to the fleet. From 1981 she was back on the Tobermory to Mingary service until she was made redundant by the car ferries and sold in 1985.

At the commissioning of *Loch Arkaig* in 1960 it was announced that three new car ferries were to be built for the services of David MacBrayne Ltd. The ferries were owned by the Secretary of State for Scotland and registered at Leith. Each appeared in 1964, *Hebrides*, on a new route linking Uig to Lochmaddy and Tarbert, being the first to enter service. She remained in service until sold in 1985 to operate from Torquay to the Channel Islands. *Clansman* was the second to enter service, from Mallaig to Armadale, and *Columba* the third, from Oban to Craignure and Lochaline. All three were identical, with lift-loading of cars, like the ABC ferries of 1964 on the Clyde although unlike the Clyde vessels, the lift was forward of the passenger accommodation.

All had cabins with sleeping berths for fifty-one passengers below the car deck. Initially these were used for inclusive tour passengers as, at that time, MacBrayne's were operating a range of bus tours from Glasgow to the West Highlands and Islands. It is claimed that these cabins were designed for the use of government officials in the event of a nuclear attack, 1964 being the height of the Cold War.

Clansman was also used on overnight trips from Mallaig to Castlebay, and to Lochboisdale. She also saw relief work on the Mallaig–Kyle–Stornoway service, and replaced *Hebrides* out of Uig. In 1973 she was converted to bow- and stern-loading, and was then briefly on the Ullapool to Stornoway service. She was then mainly on the Ardrossan to Arran route until sold in 1984.

From 1975, *Columba* was on a variety of trips out of Oban: to Staffa and Iona twice weekly, replacing *King George V*, to Coll and Tiree and to Colonsay, each thrice weekly. These sailings could be combined as a mini-cruise. In 1979 and 1980 she sailed to St Kilda, non-landing, at the beginning of the season. These sailings from Oban lasted until 1988. In the following year she was sold to Hebridean Island Cruises and converted to the luxury cruise ship *Hebridean Princess*, sailing on cruises around the west coast of Scotland each year since.

In 1965 the turntable car ferry *Maid of Glencoe* was taken over and renamed *Scalpay* for the Kyles Scalpay to Scalpay ferry service, a new route introduced after the withdrawal of the Outer Isles mail steamer, which had called at Scalpay. She was sold in 1971.

In January 1969 the Scottish Transport Group was formed, taking over the Caledonian Steam Packet Co., the 50 per cent of David MacBrayne Ltd owned by British Railways and the nationalised Scottish Bus Group. Six months later, the remaining 50 per cent of David MacBrayne Ltd was purchased from Coast Lines Ltd.

November 1969 saw the transfer of the CSP car ferry *Arran* to MacBrayne for the Tarbert to Islay route. She was altered to stern-loading in the winter of 1972/3 and was replaced by the new *Pioneer* on the route in 1974, when she returned to the Clyde.

The car ferry *Iona* was built in 1970 and was intended for the Islay service. A plan to build a new pier at Redhouse, south of Kennacraig, was cancelled and the resulting inability to use the pier at West Loch Tarbert meant that she was unable to be used there and she entered service under CSP colours on the Gourock to Dunoon service. In 1972 she was moved to the West Highlands, serving on a number of different routes, and inaugurated the car ferry service from Ullapool to Stornoway in 1973. In 1975 she was rebuilt, with a new deckhouse with cabins on the upper deck replacing her dummy funnel; and her exhausts, previously white, repainted as funnels; and was placed on the route from Oban to Castlebay and Lochboisdale. In 1979 she was moved to her originally intended route from Kennacraig, which had by then replaced West Loch Tarbert, to Islay. In 1997 she was sold to Pentland Ferries for service from Gills Bay, Caithness, to St Margaret's Hope in Orkney and renamed *Pentalina B*.

The year 1971 saw the arrival of a second *Scalpay* for the Scalpay service. She had been built in 1956 for the Kyle of Lochalsh to Kyleakin route as *Lochalsh*. She was replaced by *Kilbrannan* in 1977 and was sold two years later.

In 1972, *Kilbrannan*, the first of what would be a series of eight Islands-class landing craft type ferries affectionately known by some in the enthusiast fraternity as 'daft ducks', entered service. She ran from Lochranza on Arran to Claonaig on the Kintyre peninsula and, although owned by David MacBrayne Ltd, carried a yellow Caledonian Steam Packet funnel until the formation of Caledonian MacBrayne in the following year. She was sold in 1992 for use on the service from Burtonport to Aranmore in County Donegal in the Republic of Ireland.

The second of this class, *Morvern*, was launched on 18 December 1972 and did not come into service until after the formation of Caledonian MacBrayne Ltd.

On 1 January 1973 David MacBrayne Ltd and the Caledonian Steam Packet Co. Ltd were merged to form Caledonian MacBrayne, the ships of which will form a later volume in this series. David MacBrayne Ltd continued to operate the remaining cargo vessels *Lochdunvegan* and *Loch Carron*, which were not repainted in the new funnel colours. Neither were *Loch Seaforth*, *Loch Arkaig* or *Claymore*, which was laid up for most of her remaining period before sale; these remained under the ownership of David MacBrayne Ltd along with *Loch Toscaig*, *Lochnell* and *Scalpay*.

The name David MacBrayne Ltd was reactivated in 2006 as the name of the holding company of the various companies in the CalMac group, including those that own the ships, the infrastructure and the operating company, and also Northlink Ferries until their contract was won by Serco in 2012.

Above: Hebrides (1898) at Loch Skipport Pier, South Uist, in a postcard view.

Right: Hebrides laid up in Albert Harbour, Greenock, in 1955.

Below: Hebrides at Carbost, Skye *c.* 1912.

Above left: *Dunara Castle* (1875) berthed at Lancefield Quay in Glasgow.

Above right: *Challenger* (1897) in the River Clyde, passing Dalmuir.

Below right: *Lochbroom* (1945) in East India Harbour, Greenock.

Above: The second *Lochbuie* (1942) arriving at Tobermory with the short-lived pale blue hull, used from 1960 to 1962 on the small vessels of the fleet.

Right: *Lochbuie* arriving at Tobermory, with the deck of *Lochearn* in the foreground and the Coast Lines cruise ship *Lady Killarney* anchored in the background.

Top left: Loch Frisa (1948) in the River Clyde off Dalmuir.

Top right: Lochdunvegan arriving at Oban on 28 July 1973 while on the Tiree car ferry service.

Bottom right: Lochdunvegan (1949) in the Clyde, off Erskine Hospital.

Top left: Loch Carron (1950) off Kerrera.

Top right: Loch Carron at her Glasgow berth in the early fifties with the bow of the short-lived Campbeltown cargo vessel *Taransay* to the left.

Bottom left: Loch Carron off Lochboisdale.

Top left: Lochshiel (1953) at Coll in 1964 with the launch *Coll* (1951) alongside.

Top right: Lochailort (1954) berthed at Acharacle in her final season, 1967.

Bottom right: Claymore (1955), with the ubiquitous Milanda bread van and some cars on the foredeck, off Tiree.

Claymore at Colonsay in 1974. Note the highlander crest on the bow.

Loch Ard (1955) in the Kingston Dock. Note the barrels on the quayside, which are probably empty whisky barrels to be returned to an island distillery.

Loch Ard lying at Port Askaig, *c.* 1960.

Above left: Loch Toscaig (1949) arrives at Kyle of Lochalsh in her light blue livery.

Above right: A cargo of sheep on *Loch Arkaig.*

Left: Loch Arkaig (1942) arriving at Armadale.

Above left: Loch Eynort (1947) during her brief spell of service.

Above right: Applecross (1944) off Iona in July 1979.

Right: The 'wee red boats' *Applecross*, *Craignure* (1943) and *Iona* (1962), moored at the slipway at Iona.

Above left: Clansman berthed at Tower Pier, on a promotional visit to London, on 9 January 1969.

Above right: Hebrides and the rebuilt *Clansman* lying in the James Watt Dock, Greenock.

Right: Columba (1964) arriving at Mallaig on 26 June 1974 in her then-new CalMac funnel colours.

Opposite top left: The cover of a preliminary leaflet about the new car ferries of 1964, with an artist's impression of them.

Opposite top right: Clansman (1964) departing from Mallaig in her original condition.

Opposite bottom left: Hebrides (1964) at Tarbert, Harris.

Opposite bottom right: Clansman and *Columba* under construction at the Hall Russell yard at Aberdeen.

Above left: The second *Scalpay*, ex *Lochalsh* (1956), arriving at Tarbert, on an occasion when the slipway at Kyles Scalpay was unavailable.

Above right: Iona (1970) in her original condition with the small central funnel.

Left: Arran (1954) at West Loch Tarbert Pier.

Kilbrannan (1972) in 2013 as *Clew Bay Queen*, loading cargo at Roonagh Quay for Clare Island and/or Inishturk.

Morvern (1973) in 2013 at Burtonport, Co. Donegal.

Chapter 6

MACBRAYNE TIMETABLES AND OTHER PUBLICITY MATERIAL

There follows a selection of timetable and guidebook covers, etc. over the years.

An 1855 advertisement for David Hutcheson & Co.'s steamer services.

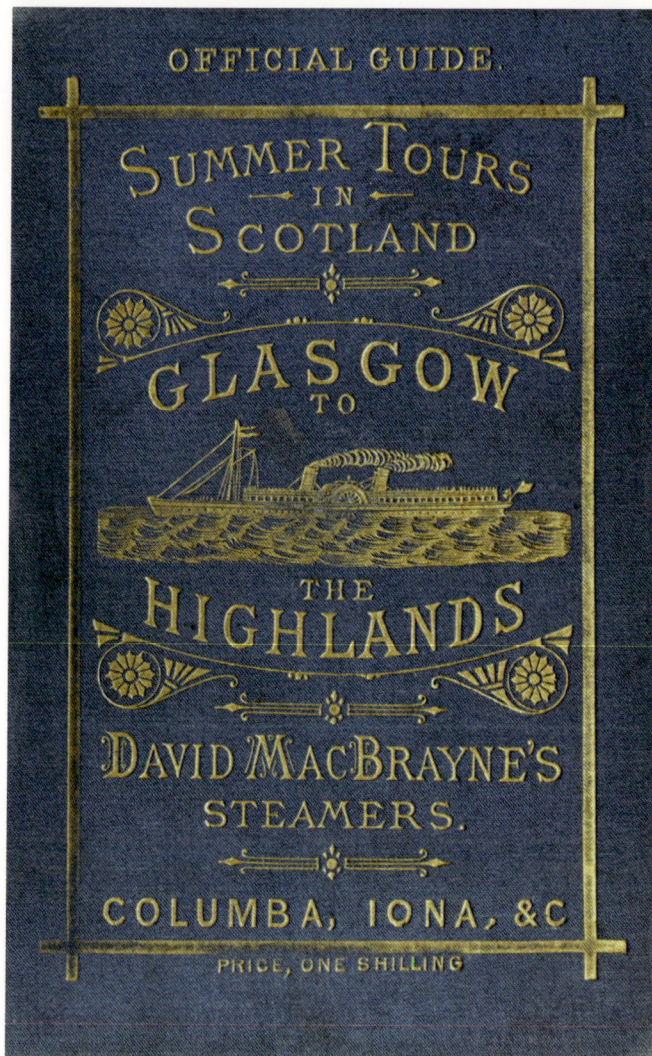

Left: The cover of the 1884 hardback MacBrayne's guidebook.

Right: The cover of the 1898 hardback edition of MacBrayne's guidebook and timetables featuring *Columba.*

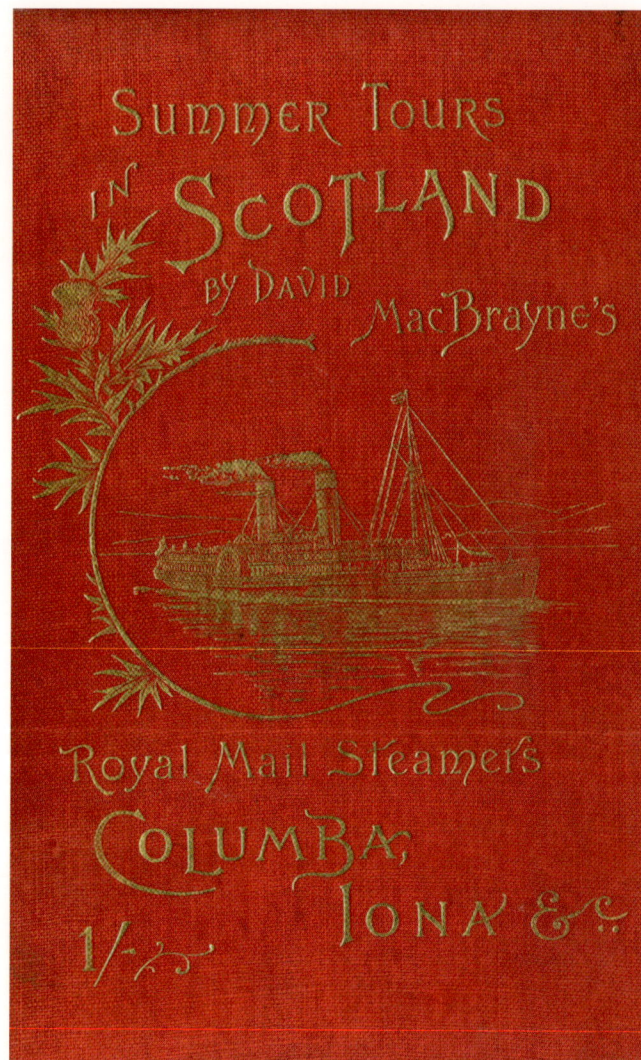

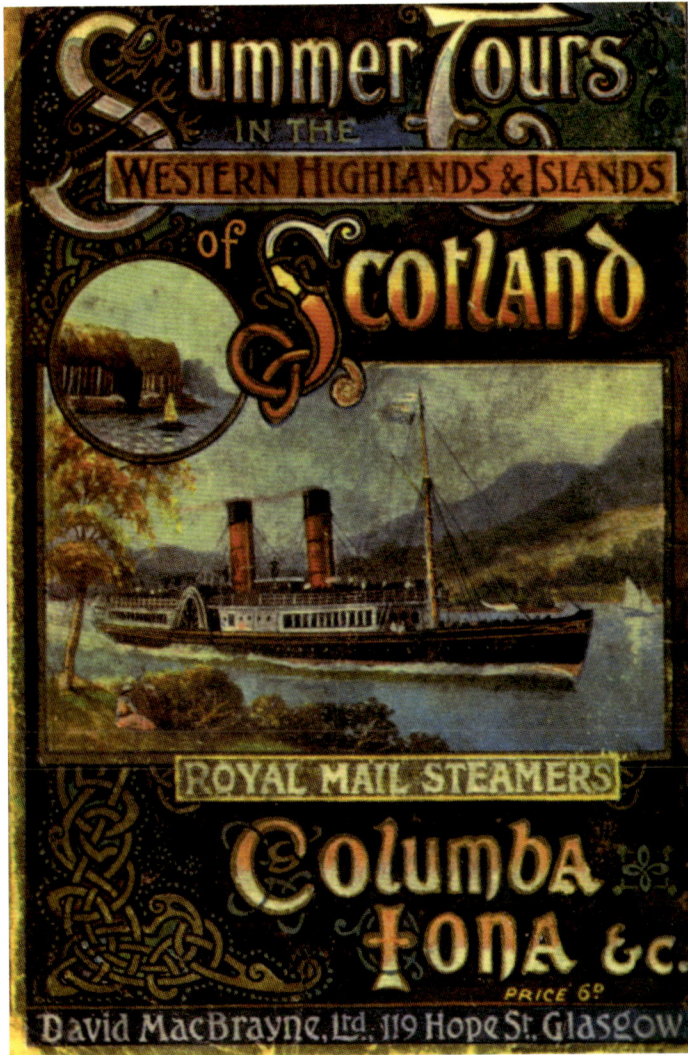

Left: The cover of a paperback edition of the 1908 MacBrayne guidebook featuring RMS *Columba*.

Right: The cover of the 1928 MacBrayne timetable.featuring RMS *Columba* in an Art Deco design.

Left: The cover of the 1935 MacBrayne timetable, featuring *Lochfyne* and a bus.

Right: The cover of the 1938 MacBrayne timetable, featuring *Lochfyne* and a group of kilted highlanders with flags. The flag theme with the fake MacBrayne pennant would continue until 1970 (fake because it was a copy of the ships' name pennants, although the one reading 'MacBraynes' was never flown from a masthead, but only used in advertising).

The cover of the 1951 centenary timetable.

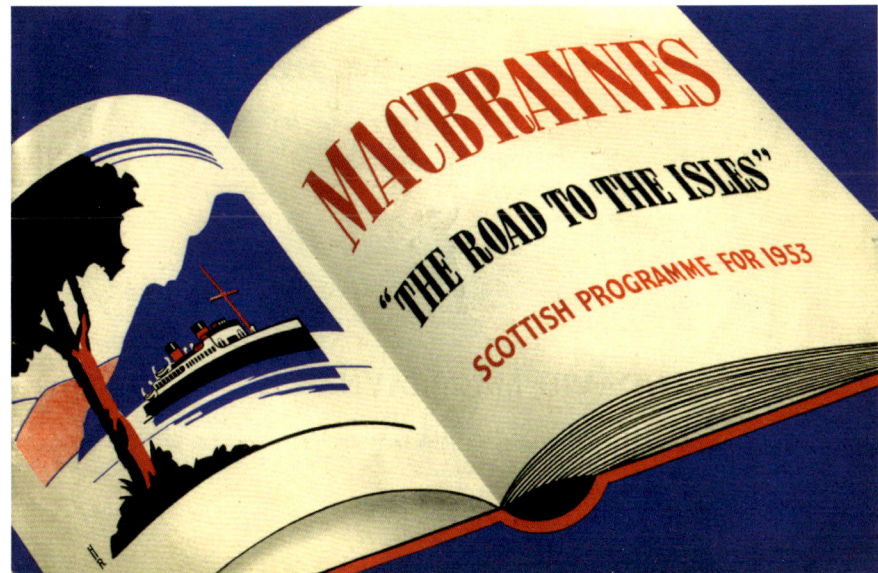

The cover of the 1953 timetable.

Above left: The cover of the 1956 timetable featuring the 1955 *Claymore*.

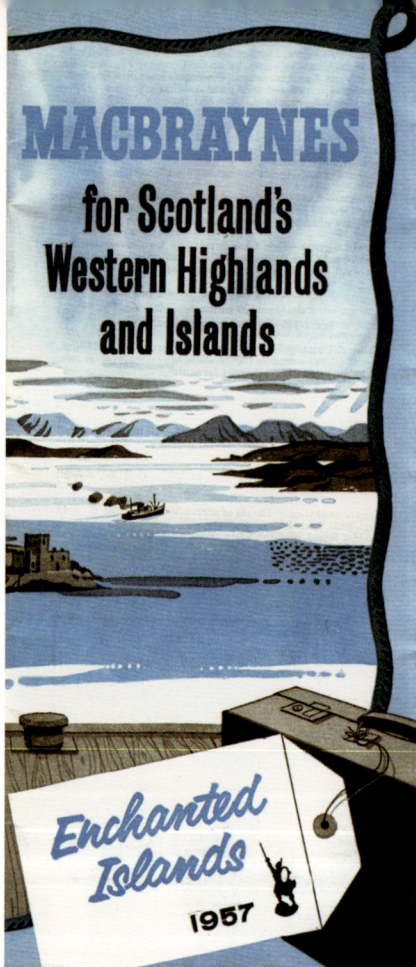

Middle: The cover of the 1957 timetable.

Above right: The cover of the 1962 timetable, duplicating that of 1938, only with *Claymore* replacing *Lochfyne*. This was repeated in 1963 and 1964, on larger format (13 inches by 9.5 inches) publications.

MACBRAYNES WINTER SERVICES TIME TABLES

2nd OCTOBER 1972 to 28th APRIL 1973

(cancelling all previous issues)

DAVID MACBRAYNE LIMITED

David MacBrayne Ltd's final timetable, for winter 1972 to 1973. The winter timetable covers were always far more plain, with just line drawings on them.

MACBRAYNES STEAMERS
Incorporating the Services of McCALLUM ORME & Co., Ltd.

CARGO SAILINGS FROM   **GLASGOW & GREENOCK**

JANUARY, 1948 (Weather and circumstances permitting).

BY THE FOLLOWING OR OTHER STEAMERS.

M.V. "LOCHSHIEL"

LOADING BERTH - 4 KINGSTON DOCK   2nd, 12th and 22nd JANUARY

To Port Ellen, Gigha, Luing, Oban, Lismore, Kingairloch, Kinlochleven, Fort William, Tobermory, Mingarry, Glenborrodale, Glencirspesdale, Laudale, Strontian, Salen-Loch Sunart. On 22nd Calls also Ardlussa, Croggan, Calgary, Ulva, Gometra, Tavool, Tiroran.

S.S. "LOCHDUNVEGAN"

LOADING BERTH - 4 KINGSTON DOCK   7th, 14th, 21st and 28th JANUARY

To Islay and Jura. To Gigha (via Port Ellen).

S.S. "ULSTER STAR"

LOADING BERTH - 6 KINGSTON DOCK   6th, 13th, 20th and 27th JANUARY

To Tobermory, Drimnin, Kilchoan, Portree, Raasay, and Stornoway.

S.S. "LOCHGORM"

LOADING BERTH - 6 KINGSTON DOCK   8th, 19th and 29th JANUARY

To Oban, Craignure, Lochaline, Salen, (Mull), Tobermory, Drimnin, Kilchoan, Eigg, Mallaig, Armadale, Glenelg, Kyle of Lochalsh, Raasay, Portree, Gairloch, Aultbea, Scorraig, Ullapool, Baden-Tarbet, Lochinver, Stockinish, Rodel, Canna, Rhum. On 29th calls also at Lochinchard, (Lochclash Pier).

S.S. "HEBRIDES"

LOADING BERTH - 46 LANCEFIELD QUAY   12th and 21st JANUARY

To Colonsay, Oban, Barra, Lochboisdale, Skipport, Kallin, Locheport, Lochmaddy, Tarbert, Uig, Dunvegan, Pooltiel, Portnalong, Carbost, Tobermory, Oban, Colonsay.

S.S. "CHALLENGER"

LOADING BERTH - 46 LANCEFIELD QUAY   7th, 19th and 28th JANUARY

To Colonsay, Elgoll and Soay, Dunvegan, Uig, Scalpay, Tarbert, Finsbay, Leverburgh, Lochmaddy, Kallin, Skipport, Lochboisdale, Eriskay. Barra, Colonsay, No call at Greenock

S.S. "DUNARA CASTLE"

LOADING BERTH - 46 LANCEFIELD QUAY   2nd, 8th, 15th, 22nd and 29th JANUARY

To Port Askaig, Colonsay, Oban, Tobermory, Coll, Tiree, Bunessan, Iona, Oban, Colonsay, Port Askaig.

44 ROBERTSON STREET, GLASGOW, C.2., DEC., 1947.

DAVID MACBRAYNE, LTD.
TEL: CENTRAL 9954/59.

The January 1948 cargo sailing list, including the steamers taken over from McCallum Orme, three MacBrayne steamers and the chartered *Ulster Star*.

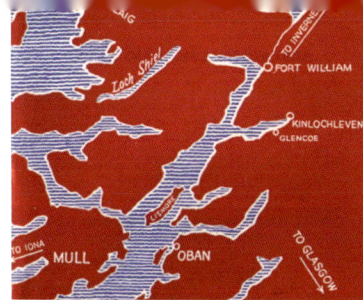

A series of regional timetable leaflets issued in the mid-1960s.

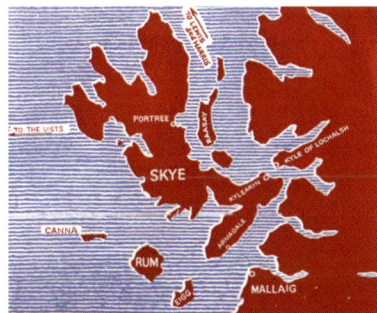

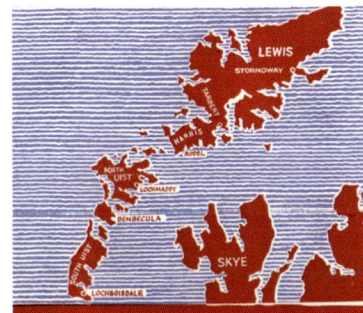

MACBRAYNE'S STEAMERS.
THE ROYAL ROUTE

CHEAP DAY EXCURSIONS
—FROM—
ROTHESAY
—TO—
KYLES OF BUTE,
TARBERT AND ARDRISHAIG
By R.M.S. "SAINT COLUMBA"
(OR OTHER STEAMER)

1ST JUNE TILL 19TH SEPT.

GOING		RETURNING	
Rothesay, leave	10-30 a.m.	Ardrishaig, leave	1-10 p.m.
Colintraive, ,,	10-55 ,,	Tarbert, ,,	1-50 ,,
Tighnabruaich, ,,	11-10 ,,	Tighnabruaich, ,,	2-50 ,,
Tarbert, ,,	12-0 Noon	Colintraive, ,,	3-5 ,,
Ardrishaig, arrive 12-45 p.m.		Rothesay, arrive	3-40 ,,

RETURN FARES:

To COLINTRAIVE or TIGHNABRUAICH (valid day of issue only)
First Class, 2/3.   Third Class, 1/6.

To TARBERT or ARDRISHAIG (valid day of issue only, or Friday or
Saturday till Tuesday).   First Class, 3/9.   Third Class, 3/-.

Tickets can be had only at MacBrayne's Office, Rothesay, or on Board Steamer
1936.   DAVID MACBRAYNE, LTD., 44 Robertson Street, Glasgow, C.2.

The Buteman, Ltd., Rothesay.

Left: A 1936 handbill for *Saint Columba*'s inaugural season from Rothesay to Ardrishaig.

Right: A 1965 handbill for the Rothesay to Ardrishaig service with *Lochfyne* and a bus tour, returning via Inveraray, Loch Eck and Dunoon.

MACBRAYNE'S STEAMERS

CHEAP DAY SAILINGS
BY

R.M.S. LOCHFYNE (or other Steamer)
TO
TARBERT & ARDRISHAIG
(via KYLES OF BUTE)
(allowing about 1½ hours ashore at Tarbert)
DAILY EXCEPT SUNDAYS ALL THE YEAR ROUND

					A	B
ROTHESAY	- Str. dep.	10 35	ARDRISHAIG - Str. dep.		13 05	12†50
TIGHNABRUAICH	,,	11 15	TARBERT - ,,		13 55	13 30
TARBERT	- ,, ,,	12 20	TIGHNABRUAICH ,,		14 50	14 25
ARDRISHAIG	,, arr.	12 55	ROTHESAY - arr.		15 30	15 05

B Until 14th May and from 1st October, Steamer terminates at Tarbert
A 15th May to 30th September.   † Coach Connection

DAY FARES—valid day of issue only		
	To Tighnabruaich (Kyles of Bute)	To Tarbert and Ardrishaig
FROM ROTHESAY	7/6	13/-

TICKETS CAN BE OBTAINED FROM THE PURSER ON BOARD THE STEAMER OR FROM
THE OFFICE ON THE PIER

CIRCULAR TOUR
BY STEAMER AND COACH TO
KYLES OF BUTE, ARDRISHAIG, INVERARAY, LOCH ECK and DUNOON
on
Mondays, Wednesdays and Fridays
31st MAY TO 10th SEPTEMBER, 1965
TIME TABLE

ROTHESAY	- Str. dep.	10 35	DUNOON	- Coach arr.	16 20
ARDRISHAIG	,, arr.	12 55	DUNOON	- Str. dep.	17 45
ARDRISHAIG	- Coach dep.	13 00	ROTHESAY	,, arr.	18 35

A short halt will be made at Inveraray.
Fare 16/-
TICKETS MUST BE OBTAINED IN ADVANCE FROM
David MacBrayne Ltd., Pier Office, Rothesay.   Phone 150

All Passengers and their Luggage, Goods and Livestock, carried subject to the Company's Conditions of Carriage as specified in Sailing Bills, Notices and Announcements.

MEALS AND REFRESHMENTS ARE AVAILABLE ON BOARD STEAMERS

DAVID MACBRAYNE LIMITED
PIER OFFICE—ROTHESAY   Phone 150

Head Office:
Clyde House
44 Robertson Street
Glasgow, C.2
Phone: CENtral 9231   SEASON 1965

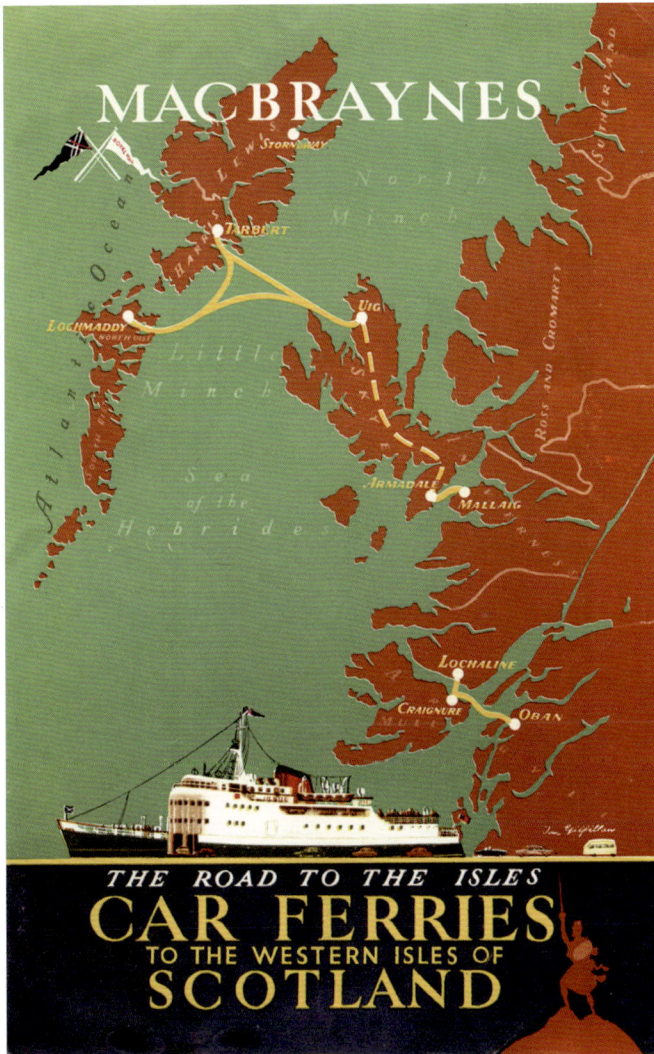

MACBRAYNES

THE ROAD TO THE ISLES
CAR FERRIES
TO THE WESTERN ISLES OF
SCOTLAND

Left: The front of a 1964 car ferry leaflet showing the inaugural timetable of the three car ferries.

Right: A handbill for the 1979 cruise by *Columba* to St Kilda.

CALEDONIAN MACBRAYNE LIMITED
CENTENARY CRUISES
By
M.V. 'Columba'
TO MARK THE FOUNDING OF
DAVID MACBRAYNE IN 1879
5th MAY — 9th MAY 1979

GOUROCK — OBAN

5th MAY — GOUROCK	Depart	0900
OBAN	Arrive	1900
Via the Mull of Kintyre		

OBAN — ST. KILDA

5th MAY — OBAN	Depart	2200
6th MAY — ST. KILDA	Arrive	1200
The vessel will circumnavigate the Islands — No landing		
ST. KILDA	Depart	1600
7th MAY — OBAN	Arrive	0600

All passengers except those continuing on Cruise F must disembark before 0815 hrs.

BOOKING FORM

Please reserve accommodation for .... passengers on Cruise ....

Please reserve space for car from Gourock:

Make .... Model .... Length ....

I enclose P.O./Cheque value £............ and agree that passengers and vehicles will be conveyed subject to the Companys Conditions of Carriage as specified in Sailing Bills, Notices and announcements.

SIGNATURE ....
NAME ....
ADDRESS ....
....

CALEDONIAN MACBRAYNE LTD.
THE FERRY TERMINAL, GOUROCK

Chapter 7

SHIP DATA

There follow some tables relating to the MacBrayne fleet..

Type	Name	Built	Entered Fleet	Disposed of	Builder	Engine Builder	Gross tons	Length	Engine type	NHP	Fate	Remarks
PS	Curlew	1837	1851	1855	David Napier, Glasgow	David Napier, Glasgow	54	95 ft	Unknown	135	Broken up 1865	
PS	Shandon	1839	1851	1853	Wood & Reid, Port Glasgow	Robert Napier, Glasgow	186	134.9 ft	Side lever	170	Broken up 1865	Wooden hull
PS	Duntroon Castle	1842	1851	1853	Anderson & Gilmour, Govan	Builder	247	140.1 ft	Steeple; 2 cylinders	130	Lost 1863	
PS	Dolphin (I)	1844	1851	1862	Rober Napier & Sons, Govan	Builder	238	170.2 ft	Steeple, single cylinder	100	Sold for blockade running 1862, wrecked 1874	
PS	Edinburgh Castle/Glengarry	1844	1851	1927	Smith & Rodger, Govan	Builder	124	138.1 ft	Steeple, single cylinder	45	Scrapped 1927	Renamed 1875, lengthened by 10.4 ft 1875
PS	Pioneer (I)	1844	1851	1895	Barr & McNab, Paisley	Builder	196	159.8 ft	Steeple, single cylinder	91	Scrapped 1895	Lengthened by 26.8 ft 1874
Track-boat	Sunbeam	1847	1851	1888	Unknown, Blackhill	n/a	n/a	80 ft	Horse-drawn	3 horses	Unknown	Overflow boat after 1866
PS	Cygnet (I)	1848	1851	1882	Wood & Reid, Port Glasgow	(1) J. & G. Thomson, Finnieston (2) Barclay, Curle & Co., Whiteinch	107	77.5 ft	(Both) Steeple, single cylinder	(Both) 50	Wrecked at Lochailort 1882	Re-engined at unkown date
PS	Lapwing (I)	1848	1851	1859	John Reid & Co.	Murdoch Aitken & Co. 1835	110	82.7 ft	Steeple, single cylinder	44	Sank off Kintyre after a collision, 22 February 1859	
Track-boat	Maid of Perth	Unknown	1851	1866	Unknown, Blackhill	n/a	n/a	Unknown	Horse-drawn	3 horses	Unknown	
PS	Mountaineer (I)	1852	1852	1889	J. & G. Thomson, Govan	Builder	173	174.3 ft	Steeple, single cylinder	120	Stranded on Lady Rock, 27 September 1889	Lengthened by 9.8 ft in 1869, and by 11.5 ft in 1871
PS	Chevalier (I)	1853	1853	1854	J. & G. Thomson, Govan	Builder	329	176.9 ft	2-cylinder Simple Oscillating	180	Wrecked in the Sound of Jura, 24 November 1854	
PS	Iona (I)	1855	1855	1862	J. & G. Thomson, Govan	Builder	325	225.2 ft	2-cylinder Simple Oscillating	220	Sold for blockade running 1862, sank off Kempock Point after a collision, 2 October 1862	
PS	Inveraray Castle/Inveraray Castle	1839	1857	1895	Tod & McGregor, Mavisbank	Builder	230	136.1 ft	Steeple; 2 cylinders	100	Broken up 1892	Renamed 1862, lengthened by 3.9 ft 1857, 183.5 ft 1862 and 14.4 ft 1873
PS	Mary Jane/Glencoe	1846	1857	1931	Tod & McGregor, Meadowside	Builder	211	149.5 ft	Steeple, single cylinder	120	Scrapped 1931	Renamed 1875, lengthened by 3.5 ft 1865 and 12.4 ft 1875
PS	Maid of Lorn/Plover (I)	1849	1857	1883	T. Wingate & Co., Whiteinch	Robert Napier, Glasgow	120	82.5 ft	Steeple, single cylinder	59	Converted to a hulk 1883, scrapped 1891	Renamed 1859
PS	Duke of Argyll	1852	1857	1858	Scott Sinclair & Co., Greenock	Builder	391	166.7 ft	Single cylinder	176	Sank in Sound of Mull, 12 January 1858	
PS	Stork	1851	1858	1861	W. Denny & Bros, Dumbarton	Caird & Co., Greenock	396	190.7 ft	Unknown	100	Sold to Italy 1861, scrapped 1875	
SS	Fingal (I)	1860	1861	1861	J. & G. Thomson, Govan	Builder	352	178 ft	2-cylinder	120	Sold for blockade running 1861, converted to ironclad gunboat, lost at sea December 1869	
PS	Fairy	1861	1861	1863	J. & G. Thomson, Govan	Builder	151	149.4 ft	2-cylinder Simple Oscillating	77	Sold for blockade running 1863, then to Uruguay	
SS	Clydesdale (I)	1862	1862	1905	J. & G. Thomson, Govan	Builder	403	180.2 ft	(1) 2-cylinder (2) compound	(1) 120 (2) 128	Stranded on Lady Rock, January 1905	Engine compounded 1893, lengthened by 16.5 ft at unknown date
PS	Iona (II)	1863	1863	1863	J. & G. Thomson, Govan	Builder	368	249.2 ft	2-cylinder Simple Oscillating	180	Sold for blockade running, wrecked off Lundy, 2 February 1864	
SS	Staffa (I)	1863	1863	1886	J. & G. Thomson, Govan	(1) Builder (2) Barclay Curle & Co., Whiteinch	268	148.4 ft	(1) 2-cylinder (2) compound	100	Ran aground off Gigha, 23 August 1886	Re-engined 1873
PS	Iona (III)	1864	1864	1935	J. & G. Thomson, Govan	Builder	393	255.5 ft	2-cylinder Simple Oscillating	180	Scrapped April 1936	
PS	Chevalier (II)	1866	1866	1927	J. & G. Thomson, Govan	Builder	302	211 ft	2-cylinder Simple Oscillating	150	Ran aground on Barmore Island, Loch Fyne, 25 March 1927	
PS	Gondolier	1866	1866	1939	J. & G. Thomson, Govan	Builder	173	148.2 ft	2-cylinder Simple Oscillating	80	Sold to the Admiralty 1940, hull sunk as a blockship in Scapa Flow	

SS	Linnet	1866	1866	1929	J. & G. Thomson, Govan	Builder	34	96 ft	2 x 2-cylinder inverted engines	50 IHP	Sold 1929, converted to a hulk, wrecked January 1932	
PS	Dolphin (II)	1849	1868	1868	Tod & McGregor, Meadowside	Builder	320	167 ft	2-cylinder	160	Sold 1868, again 1870 and 1872	Ex-*Islay*, 1868
SS	Clansman (I)	1870	1870	1909	J. & G. Thomson, Govan	Builder	600	211.3 ft	Compound	150	Broken up 1910	
SS	Queen of the Lake	1863	1876	1882	Duncan Young, Bravallich, Port Sonachan	A. Campbell & Son	51	80 ft	2-cylinder	15	Hulked 1882	
SS	Lochawe	1876	1876	1924	A. & J. Inglis, Pointhouse	Muir & Caldwell, Glasgow	97	100.2 ft	2-cylinder	30	Scrapped 1924	
PS	Islay (I)	1867	1877	1890	Barclay, Curle & Co., Glasgow	Builder	362	192.7 ft	Steeple; 2 cylinders	145	Wrecked at Red Bay, Co. Antrim December 1890	Lengthened by 13.9 ft, 1882
SS	Fingal (II)	1877	1877	1917	A. & J. Inglis, Pointhouse	Muir & Caldwell, Glasgow	124	115.3 ft	Compound	30 RHP	Sold January 1917, sunk September 1917	Intended to be named *Lochness*, renamed before completion
SS	Lochiel (I)	1877	1877	1907	A. & J. Inglis, Pointhouse	Muir & Caldwell, Glasgow	262	139.8 ft	Compound	50	Ran ashore 1907	
PS	Columba (I)	1878	1878	1936	J. & G. Thomson, Clydebank	Builder	543	301.4 ft	2-cylinder Simple Oscillating	351	Scrapped April 1936	
SS	Cavalier	1881	1881	1919	Aitken & Mansel, Glasgow	Muir & Caldwell, Glasgow	369	151.1 ft	Compound	113	Sold 1919, broken up 1927	
SS	Claymore (I)	1881	1881	1931	J. & G. Thomson, Clydebank	Builder	726	227 ft	Compound	308	Scrapped 1931	
PS	Lochness (I)	1853	1885	1912	J. Barr, Kelvinhaugh	Builder	121	153 ft	Steeple, single cylinder	80	Scrapped 1912	Ex *Lough Foyle*, ex *Lochgoil*
SS	Ethel/Clansman (II)	1880	1885	1916	Workman, Clark & Co., Belfast	J. Rowan & Sons, Glasgow	281	150.1 ft	Compound	60	Sold 1916, sank 22 October 1924	Renamed 1910
PS	Grenadier	1885	1885	1928	J. & G. Thomson, Clydebank	Builder	372	222.9 ft	Compound Oscillating	200	Burnt out 5/6 September 1927, then scrapped	
SS	Gladiator	1860	1887	1893	M. Pearse & Co., Stockton-on-Tees	Dunsmuir & Jackson, Govan	659	192.8 ft	Compound	80	Sank 12 December 1893	
PS/SS	Countess of Kellie	1869	1887	1904	A. Stephen & Sons, Kelvinhaugh	Muir & Caldwell, Glasgow	68	81.1 ft	(1) unknown (2) compound	(1) 30 (2) 95	Unknown	Converted from paddle to screw 1887
SS	Udea	1873	1887	1894	Schlesinger, Davis & Co., Wallsend	(1) Christie, Gutch & Co., North Shields (2) unknown	157	110.5 ft	(1) 2-cylinder (2) compund	30	Sank 7 April 1894	Re-engined 1892
SS	Handa	1878	1887	1917	Blackwood & Gordon, Port Glasgow	Builder	146	84.2' ft	Compound	35 RHP	Sold for scrapping, abandoned at sea 24 December 1917	Ex *Aros Castle*
SS	Pelican	1850	1888	1895	E. Pike, Cork	J. Dickinson, Sunderland	638	205.6 ft	Compound	140	Wrecked, 6 December 1898	
SS	Falcon	1854	1888	1890	E. Pike, Cork	Palmer's Shipbuilding Co., Jarrow	613	211 ft	Compound	100	Abandoned at sea, December 1890	
SS	Staffa (II)	1861	1888	1909	W. Simons & Co., Renfrew	Portillo White & Co., Seville	211	141.8 ft	Compound	60 RHP	Scrapped 1909	Ex-*Adela*, shortened by 7.3 ft 1891, had been re-engined 1870
PS	Fusilier	1888	1888	1934	McArthur & Co., Paisley	Hutson & Corbett, Glasgow	251	202 ft	Single cylinder diagonal	133	Sold 1934, scrapped October 1939	
SS	Margaret	Unknown	1888	1894	D. M. Cumming, Blackhill	Builder	60	66.5 ft	Unknown	25	Sold 1894, no fate recorded	
SS	Loanda	1870	1889	1897	J. Elder & Co., Govan	Builder	1,475	279.1 ft	Compound	221	Scrapped 1897	
TSS	Flowerdale	1878	1889	1904	Barrow Shipbuilding Co., Barrow	Builder	488	177 ft	2 x compound	150	Lost off Lismore 1904, engines and boilers salved and reused	Ex-*Recovery*
SS	Texa	1884	1889	1917	Scott & Co., Bowling	W. King & Co., Glasgow	157	100 ft	Compound	35	Sold 1917, wrecked April 1932	Ex-*James Mutter*, lengthened by 18.4 ft 1891
PS	Hero/Mountaineer (II)	1858	1890	1909	T. Wingate & Co., Whiteinch	Builder	157	181 ft	Steeple, single cylinder	80	Sold for scrapping 1909	Renamed 1892
PS	Islay (II)	1872	1890	1902	Tod & McGregor, Meadowside	Builder	497	211.4 ft	Steeple; 2 cylinders	200	Ran aground 15 July 1902	Ex-*Princess Louise*
PS	Cygnus/Brigadier	1854	1891	1896	J. Henderson & Sons, Renfrew	McNab & Clark, Greenock	250	182 ft	2-cylinder Simple Oscillating	120	Wrecked 7 December 1896	Renamed 1892
PS	Great Western/Lovedale	1862	1891	1904	W. Simons & Co., Renfrew	Builder	466	220.4 ft	2-cylinder Simple Oscillating	190	Broken up 1904	Renamed 1893
PS	Gael	1867	1891	1925	Robertson & Co., Greenock	Rankin & Blackmore, Greenock	419	211 ft	2-cylinder Simple Oscillating	150	Broken up 1924	
PS	Carabinier	1878	1893	1909	Oswald Mordaunt & Co., Southampton	Builder	269	169.4 ft	Compound Oscillating	120	Broken up 1908	Ex-*Albert Edward*
SS	Maud	Unknown	1889	1897	T. B. Seath & Co., Rutherglen	Builder	10	Unknown	Unknown	10	Unknown	
PS	Gairlochy	1861	1894	1919	Barclay Curle & Co., Glasgow	Barclay Curle & Co., Whiteinch	124	176 ft	Steeple, single cylinder	60	Destroyed by fire 24 December 1919	Ex-*Ardmore*, ex-*Sultan*, shortened by 27.7 ft 1895

SS	Hibernian	1875	1894	1894	H. Murrray & Co., Port Glasgow	Kemp & Hume, Glasgow	334	145.3 ft	Compound	47	Lost after collision 12 April 1894	
SS	Aggie (chartered)	1893	1894	1907	J. Fullerton & Co., Paisley	Ross & Duncan, Glasgow	183	110.2 ft	Compound	45 RHP	Unknown	
PS	Glendale	1875	1902	1905	J. Elder & Co., Govan	Builder	481	220 ft	Compound Oscillating	335	Ran aground 20 July 1905	Ex-*La Belgique*, ex-*Flamingo*, ex-*Paris*
SS	Lapwing (II)	1903	1903	1918	Scott & Co., Bowling	Hutson & Sons	211	135.2 ft	Compound	64 RHP	Sold 1918, scarped 1931	Later *Cowal*
SS	Brenda	1904	1904	1929	Scott & Co., Bowling	J. Fisher & Co., Paisley	115	82 ft	Compound	20 RHP	Scrapped 1929	Engine built 1888, formerly in a yacht
SS	Cygnet (II)	1904	1904	1930	A. & J. Inglis, Pointhouse	Barrow Shipbuilding Co. Ltd	191	135 ft	Compound	72 RHP	Sold for breaking up 1930	Engine built 1878, formerly starboard engine in *Flowerdale*
SS	Plover (II)/Loch Aline	1904	1904	1946	Scott & Co., Bowling	Barrow Shipbuilding Co. Ltd	208	136.8 ft	Compound	77 RHP	Sold 1947, scrapped 1951	Renamed 1934, engine built 1878, formerly port engine in *Flowerdale*
SS	Sheila	1904	1904	1927	A. & J. Inglis, Pointhouse	Builder	280	150.2 ft	Triple expansion	76 RHP	Wrecked 1 January 1927	
SS	Clydesdale (II)	1905	1905	1953	Scott & Co., Bowling	Ross & Duncan, Glasgow	394	151.1 ft	Triple expansion	85 RHP	Sold for breaking up 1953	
PS	Pioneer (II)	1905	1905	1945	A. & J. Inglis, Pointhouse	Builder	241	160 ft	Compound Diagonal	84	Sold to the Admiralty 1945, scrapped 1958	Renamed HMS *Harbinger* 1945
TSMV	Comet	1905	1907	1947	A. W. Robertson & Co., Canning Town, London	(1 and 2) L. Gardner & Sons, Manchester	43	65 ft	(1) 2 x 4-cylinder paraffin motors (2) 2 x 8-cylinder semi-diesels	(1) 120 (2) 180 BHP	Sold 1947, later converted to a houseboat, still in existence	Ex-*Win*
SS	Chieftain	1907	1907	1919	Ailsa Shipbuilding Co. Ltd, Troon	Clyde Shipbuilding & Engineering Co. Ltd, Port Glasgow	1,081	241.7 ft	Triple expansion	257	Sold 1919, scrapped 1952	Later *St Margaret*, *Prince Charles*, *Camosun* and *Cairo*
TSMV	Scout	1907	1907	1913	Ailsa Shipbulding Co. Ltd, Troon	Griffin Engineering Co. Ltd, Bath	82	100 ft	2 x 4-cylinder paraffin motors	260 IHP	Destroyed by fire 19/8/1913	
SS	Nellie/Staffa (III)	1892	1908	1916	J. H. Gilmour, Irvine	Muir & Houston	89	80 ft	Compound	25	Renamed 1910, sold 1916, scrapped 1947	Renamed 1910
SS	Lochiel (II)	1908	1908	1918	Scott & Sons, Bowling	Ross & Duncan, Glasgow	241	135.4 ft	Compound	74 RHP	Sunk by a U-boat, 24 July 1918	
TrSMV/TSMV	Lochinvar	1908	1908	1960	Scott & Sons, Bowling	(1 and 2) L. Gardner & Sons, Manchester (3) Davey, Pasman & Co., (Colchester) Ltd	178	145.2 ft	(1) 3 x 6-cylinder paraffin motors (2) 3 x 4-cylinder oil engines (3) 2 x 6-cylinder diesel	(1) 288 BHP (2) 64 (3) 330 BHP	Sold 1960, wrecked 3 April 1966	Re-engined 1926 and 1949, converted from triple screw to twin screw 1949, later named *Anzio I*
SS	Dirk	1909	1909	1918	Scott & Sons, Bowling	Ross & Duncan, Glasgow	181	125.3 ft	Compound	70 RHP	Sunk by a U-boat, 29 May 1918	
PS	Mountaineer (III)	1910	1910	1938	A. & J. Inglis, Pointhouse	Builder	235	190 ft	Compound Diagonal	235	Broken up 1938	
TSS	Loch Leven Queen/Lochness (II)	1896	1911	1929	Russell & Co., Port Glasgow	Muir & Houston	82	87.1 ft	2 x compound	20	Sold for scrapping, 1929	Ex-*Lough Neagh Queen*, ex-*Clutha No. 12*, renamed 1912
MV	Cona	1906	1911	c. 1917	James Adam & Sons, Gourock	Albion Motors Ltd	n/a	35 ft	2-cylinder motor	Unknown	Unknown	Wooden hull
TSS	Duke of Abercorn	1888	1914	1915	Grangemouth Dockyard Co. Ltd	Hawthorn & Co., Leith	144	120.4 ft	2 x compound	50 RHP	Scrapped 1915	Ex-*Brittania*
SS	Kate	1894	1914	1917	Unknown, Bristol	Unknown	18	60.1 ft	Unknown	11	Sold 1917	
SS	Countess of Mayo	1897	1914	1917	T. B. Seath & Co., Rutherglen	J. Fisher & Co., Paisley	46	70.2 ft	Compound	90 IHP	Sold 1917, final fate unknown	Later named *Walker*
SS	Lochiel (III)	1906	1919	1938	Scott of Kinghorn Ltd	Builder	314	140.2 ft	Compound	52 RHP	Sold 1938	Ex *Devonia*
MV	Lochgorm (I)/Iona (IV)	1913	1928	1938	Dan Marine Motor & Shipbulding Co., Ipswich	Penman & Co. Ltd, Glasgow	37	60.3 ft	Unknown	45 BHP	Hull sold 1938	Ex *C & B No. 1*, renamed 1936
SS	Lochdunvegan (I)	1891	1929	1948	Caird & Co., Greenock	Builders	411	175.4 ft	Triple expansion	85 RHP	Scrapped 1948	Ex *Denbigh Coast*, ex *Kelvindale*, ex *Grouse*
TSS	Lochness (III)	1929	1929	1955	Harland & Wolff Ltd, Govan	J. G. Kincaid & Co. Ltd, Greenock	777	200.3 ft	2 x Triple Expanson	150	Sold 1955, scrapped 1974	
MV	Lochshiel (I)	1929	1929	1952	H. Robb Ltd, Leith	L. Gardner & Sons Ltd, Manchester	208	105.8 ft	6-cylinder diesel	300 BHP	Sold 1952, broken up 1955	
TSMV	Lochearn	1930	1930	1952	Ardrossan Dockyard Ltd	(1) L. Gardner & Sons Ltd, Manchester (2) Daey, Paxman & Co. (Colchester) Ltd	542	155.7 ft	(1) 2 x 12-cylinder diesels (2) 4 x 24-cylinder diesels	(1) 600 BHP (2) 660 BHP	Sold 1964, broken up by early 1970s	Re-engined 1948

Type	Name				Builder	Engine builder	Tonnage	Length	Engine	Power	Fate	Notes
TSMV	Lochmor	1930	1930	1952	Ardrossan Dockyard Ltd	(1) L. Gardner & Sons Ltd, Manchester (2) Davey, Paxman & Co. (Colchester) Ltd	542	155.7 ft	(1) 2 x 12-cylinder diesels (2) 4 x 24-cylinder diesels	(1) 600 BHP (2) 660 BHP	Sold 1964, broken up by early 1970s	Re-engined 1949
SS	Lochbroom (I)	1871	1931	1937	J. Elder & Co., Govan	Builder	1,139	241.9 ft	Compound	1,800 IHP	Broken up 1937	Ex *City of London*
TSMV	Lochfyne	1931	1931	1970	W. Denny & Bros Ltd, Dumbarton	(1) Daviey Paxman & Co. Ltd (2) British Polar Engines Ltd, Glasgow	748	209.9 ft	(1) 2 x 5-cylinder 4-stroke diesels (2) 2 x 8-cylinder diesels	2,000 IHP	Sold 1970, scrapped 1974	Re-engined 1953
SS	Princess Louise	1898	1934	1939	Ritchie, Graham & Milne, Whiteinch	Campbell & Calderwood, Paisley	109	95.1 ft	Compound	30	Sold 1939, destroyed by bombing 7 May 1941	
TSMV	Lochnevis	1934	1934	1970	W. Denny & Bros Ltd, Dumbarton	(1) Daviey Paxman & Co. Ltd (2) National Oil & Gas Engine Co. Ltd, Ashton-under-Lyne	568	175 ft	(1) 2 x 6-cylinder diesels (2) 2 x 6-cylinder oil engines	(1) 1,300 BHP (2) 1,560 BHP	Sold 1970, scrapped 1974	Re-engined 1957
TrSS	Saint Columba	1912	1936	1958	W. Denny & Bros Ltd, Dumbarton	Builder	792	270.3 ft	3 x turbines, direct drive	3,000 SHP	Broken up 1929	
TSS	King George V	1926	1936	1975	W. Denny & Bros Ltd, Dumbarton	Parsons Marine Steam Turbine Co. Ltd, Wallsend-on-Tyne	797	260.6 ft	6 x geared turbines	3,500 SHP	Sold 1975, damaged by fire 1981 and broken up	
SS	Lochgorm (II)	1896	1937	1951	Blackwood & Gordon, Port Glasgow	Builder	635	190.5 ft	Triple expansion	126	Broken up 1951	Ex *Lairdspool*, ex *Lily*
SS	Lochgarry	1898	1937	1942	A. & J. Inglis, Pointhouse	Builder	1,670	165 ft	Triple expansion	367	Sunk 21 January 1942	Ex *Lairdsrock*, ex *Vulture*
MV	Garry	1937	1937	1969	H. McLean, Govan	The Bergius Co. Ltd, Glasgow	n/a	25 ft	Diesel	15	Sold 1969, trace lost	Wooden hull
TSMV	Lochbuie (I)	1938	1938	1947	Nicholas Witsen & Vis, Amsterdam	M. A. N. Augsburg & Nuremberg	40	59.4 ft	4 x 12-cylinder diesels	260 BHP	Sold 1947, converted to a yacht	
TSMV	Lochiel (IV)	1939	1939	1970	W. Denny & Bros Ltd, Dumbarton	Davey, Paxman & Co. (Colchester) Ltd	580	183.7 ft	4 x 16-cylinder diesels	140	Sold 1970, scrapped 1995	Later *Norwest Laird*, *Old Lochiel* and then *Lochiel* again
SS	Ulster Star (chartered)	1904	1942	1947	Ramage & Ferguson Ltd, Leith	Builder	576	186.4 ft	Triple expansion	132	Scrapped 1949	Ex *Dynamic*, ex *Lismore*, ex *Broom*, ex *James Crombie*
TSS	Robina (chartered)	1914	1946	1948	Ardrossan Dockyard Ltd	McKie & Baxter, Glasgow	306	159.6 ft	2 x Triple Expanson	79	Scrapped 1958	
TSMV	Lochnell	1941	1947	1981	J. A. Silver Ltd, Rosneath	The Bergius Co. Ltd, Glasgow	31	51.5 ft	8-cylinder diesel	60 BHP	Sold 1981, converted for private use. Still in existence at Faversham, Kent	Ex-*Galen*, wooden hull
TSMV	Loch Seaforth	1947	1947	1973	W. Denny & Bros Ltd, Dumbarton	Sulzer Bros, Wintethiur, Switzerland	1,089	229.4 ft	2 x 12-cylinder diesels	217	Ran aground 22 March 1973, scrapped 1973	
SS	Dunara Castle	1875	1948	1948	Blackwood & Gordon, Port Glasgow	Builder	423	180.4 ft	Compound	123	Scrapped 1948	
SS	Challenger	1897	1948	1948	Hall Rusell & Co. Ltd, Aberdeen	Builder	151	107.5 ft	Compound	50 RHP	Scrapped 1948	
SS	Hebrides (I)	1898	1948	1955	Ailsa Shipbulding Co. Ltd, Troon	A. & J. Inglis, Pointhouse	585	180 ft	Triple expansion	90 RHP	Scrapped 1955	
mv	Lochbroom (II)	1945	1948	1971	Scott & Sons, Bowling	British Polar Engines Ltd	413	144 ft	2 x 5-cylinder diesels	84	Sold 1971, sank September 1974	Launched as *Empire Maysong*
MV	Lochbuie (II)	1942	1949	1968	Groves & Gutteridge, East Cowes, Isle of Wight	F. Perkins Ltd, Peterbourough	33	58.1 ft	12-cylinder diesel	300 BHP	Scrapped 1968	Ex-*G S Pinnace 1213* wooden hull
MV	Loch Frisa	1948	1949	1963	Morton Eng. & Drydock Co. Ltd, Quebec, Canada	Canadian Vickers Ltd, Montreal	338	143.6 ft	Triple expansion	73 MN	Sold 1963, scrapped early 1980s	Ex-*Marleen*, launched as *Ottowa Maycliff*
MV	Lochdunvegan (II)	1948	1950	1973	Akt Lindholmens Varv, Gothenburg, Sweden	A/B Atlas Diesel, Stockholm	562	179.7 ft	5-cylinder diesel	188	Sold 1973	Ex *Örnen*
MV	Loch Carron	1950	1951	1977	Ardrossan Dockyard Ltd	British Polar Engines Ltd	650	194.8'	2 x 6-cylinder diesels	850 BHP	Sold 1977, sank in the 1980s	
MV	Rosalind/Lochshiel (II)	1953	1953	1970	J. Barr & Sons (Craigendoran) Ltd	The Bergius Co. Ltd, Glasgow	16	45.3 ft	Kelvin diesel	66 BHP	Sunk 28 April 1970	Renamed 1953
MV	Lochailort	1954	1953	1969	J. Barr & Sons (Craigendoran) Ltd	The Bergius Co. Ltd, Glasgow	14	45.3 ft	Kelvin diesel	66 BHP	Burnt deliberately 1969	

MV	Loch Toscaig	1949	1955	1975	J. Bolson & Co., Poole	The Bergius Co. Ltd, Glasgow	49	61 ft	diesel	132	Sold 1975, later wrecked, wreck removed 1986	
TSMV	Claymore (II)	1955	1955	1976	W. Denny & Bros Ltd, Dumbarton	Builder	1,024	185.5 ft	2 x 8-cylinder diesels	1,130 BHP	Sold 1976, sank in lay-up 2000	
MV	Loch Ard	1955	1955	1971	Ferguson Bros (Port Glasgow) Ltd	British Polar Engines Ltd	611	175.6 ft	2 x 6-cylinder diesels	1,000 BHP	Sold 1971, sank 7 May 1984	
TSMV	Loch Arkaig	1942	1959	1979	J. Bolson & Co., Poole	The Bergius Co. Ltd, Glasgow	130	113 ft	2 x 8-cylinder diesels	240 BHP	Sold 1979, sank 28 October 1985	Former inshore minesweeper wooden hlull
MV	Loch Eynort	1947	1961	1971	Wivenhoe Shipyards Ltd, Wivenhoe, Essex	Crossley Bros Ltd, Manchester	135	91.5 ft	2 x 4-cylinder diesels	240 BHP	Sold 1971, converted to a yacht	Ex-*Valonia* wooden hull
MV	Applecross	1944	1963	1988	Timbacraft Ltd, Shandon	The Bergius Co. Ltd, Glasgow	n/a	40 ft	Kelvin diesel	Unknown	Abandoned 1980s	Wooden hull, ex-*Highlander*
TSMV	Clansman (III)	1964	1964	1984	Hall Rusell & Co. Ltd, Aberdeen	Crossley Bros. Ltd, Manchester	2,104	220 ft	2 x 8-cylinder diesels	2,400 BHP	Sold 1984, abandoned off the coast of Sudan in 2002 or earlier	Converted to bow and stern loading 1973
TSMV	Columba (II)	1964	1964	1989	Hall Rusell & Co. Ltd, Aberdeen	Crossley Bros Ltd, Manchester	2,104	220 ft	2 x 8-cylinder diesels	2,400 BHP	Sold 1989, still in service as the cruise ship *Hebridean Princess*	
TSMV	Hebrides (II)	1964	1964	1985	Hall Rusell & Co. Ltd, Aberdeen	Crossley Bros Ltd, Manchester	2,104	220 ft	2 x 8-cylinder diesels	2,400 BHP	Sold 1982, scrapped 2003	
MV	Scalpay (I)	1957	1965	1971	J. Noble, Fraserburgh	Unknown	24	45.5 ft	Unknown	Unknown	Sold 1971, hull used as pontoon	Ex-*Maid of Glencoe*, wooden hull
TSMV	Arran	1953	1969	1980	W. Denny & Bros Ltd, Dumbarton	British Polar Engines Ltd	568	178.8 ft	2 x 6-cylinder diesels	393	Sold 1980, broken up 1993	Converted to stern-loading 1973
TSMV	Iona (VII)	1970	1970	1997	Ailsa Shipbulding Co. Ltd, Troon	English Electric Diesels Ltd, Paxman Engine Divison, Colchester	1,192	230 ft	2 x 12-cylinder diesels	1,600 BHP	Sold 1997, still operating	Became *Penalina B*
TSMV	Scalpay (II)	1956	1971	1979	W. Denny & Bros Ltd, Dumbarton	Glennifer Engine Co., Anniesland, Glasgow	24	40.2 ft	3-cylinder diesel	36 BHP	Sold 1979	Ex *Lochalsh II*, ex *Lochalsh*
TSMV	Kilbrannan	1972	1972	1992	James Lamont & Co., Port Glasgow	English Electric Diesels Ltd (Kelvin), Glasgow	65	63 ft	2 x 6-cylinder diesels	300 BHP	Sold 1992, still in service	Later *Arainn Mhor* and *Clew Bay Queen*
TSMV	Morvern	1972	1973	1995	James Lamont & Co., Port Glasgow	English Electric Diesels Ltd (Kelvin), Glasgow	64	63 ft	2 x 6-cylinder diesels	300 BHP	Sold 1995, still in service	

MacBrayne also operated the following small open motor boats, known as 'wee red boats' and used as ferries, also known as flit-boats, to serve the larger ships at ports where there was no pier – Iona, Staffa, Eigg, Colonsay until 1964, Coll until 1964, Craignure until 1963, Glenelg and Kilchoan/Mingary:

Mingary, later named *Kilchoan* (1931–63), *Staffa* (IV) (1932–9), *Fingal* (III) (1933–61), *Glenelg* (1933–48), *Soay* (1933–55), *Kyle* (1933–41), *Kallin* (1948–68), *Marne* (1948–67), *Craignure* (1950–79), *Iona* (V) (1950–61), *Staffa* (V) (1950–67), *Coll* (I) 1951–67, *Colonsay*, renamed *Eriskay* in 1965 (1951–69), *Ulva* (1956–2000), *Iona* (VI) (1962–88), and *Eigg* (1966–78). All were 30 to 35 feet long.

Also the following inherited from McCallum Orme Ltd, in 1948: *Arinagour* (1948–9), *Nora* (1948–9), *Eriskay* (1948–51), *Glassard* (1948–9) and *Janet B* (1948).

There were also two similar rowing boats used at Rodel and Stockinish respectively, *Dumb Barge No. 1* (1932–48) and *Dumb Barge No. 2* (1933–56), and *Dumb Barge No. 3*, a former lifeboat from Marleen/Loch Frisa which operated at Iona (1949–56).

ACKNOWLEDGEMENTS

The illustrations used here are from the author's collection. A large number are from a collection of glass slides from the estate of the late Captain Alex F. Rodger, who was in life a Cape Horner, a Clyde steamers captain and enthusiast and a native of Jordanhill, where he lived in Airthrey Avenue. His glass slides were donated to Iain Quinn, who lives in Airthrey Avenue, and returned there fifty years after they were taken to Canada. The slides were flown back to the UK and transferred to PS *Waverley* in London and steamed to Glasgow on her light voyage home in the autumn of 2000. Alex was a respected figure in retirement and was honorary president of the CRSC until his passing in the early 1970s.

Many thanks to Iain Quinn for checking the proofs and for the use of photographs from his own collection. Thanks also to Edward Quinn, Robin Love, Campbell McCutcheon and Gordon Lawe for the use of their photographs.

Other images are from photos sold at meetings of the Clyde River Steamer Club and West Highland Steamer Club over a good number of years, many from anonymous enthusiast photographers.

Special thanks is due to the Mitchell Library for use of photos from the collection there of that doyen of steamer enthusiasts, Graham Easton Langmuir (1910–94). This marvellous collection contains photographs of many tens of thousands of steamers and motor vessels which have operated on the UK coast.

Thanks are also due to the staff at Paisley Photoshop who have printed some of the images.

Most of the historical information and ship data comes from *West Highland Steamers* by C. L. D. Duckworth and G. E. Langmuir, Fourth Edition, published by Brown, Son & Ferguson, Glasgow, 1987.

Want to find out more about the steamers and piers of the West Highlands?
Join the West Highland Steamer Club
Introductory Offer: Only £10 for first year's subscription
Two Newsletters a year with the tiniest details of the various CalMac ships' movements and occasional articles on long-gone steamers
Meetings in Glasgow monthly from October until April
Please send subscriptions to the treasurer, Robin Love, 29 Cyprus Ave, Elderslie, Renfrewshire, PA5 8NB, Quoting 'MS-IH'.